The Egyptian Department
and its excavations

by Dows Dunham
Curator Emeritus of Egyptian Art

Museum of Fine Arts

Boston

Contents

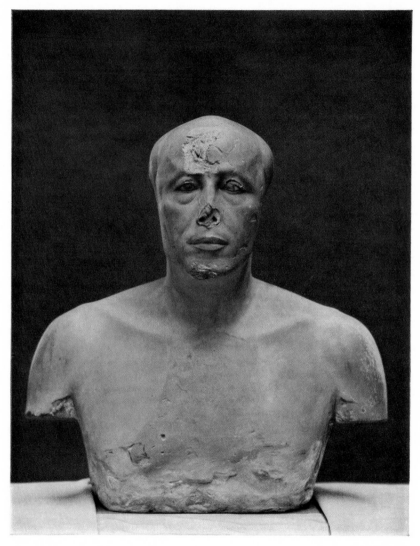

26. Limestone portrait bust of Prince Ankh-haf, plastered and painted.
H. 1 ft. 8 in. 4th Dynasty. From his tomb at Giza. *Expedition.*

THIS MONOGRAPH IS ADAPTED FROM A SERIES OF LECTURES ON THE HIS-
TORY OF THE EGYPTIAN DEPARTMENT AND THE EXCAVATIONS IN EGYPT
OF THE HARVARD-BOSTON EXPEDITION, GIVEN IN THE MUSEUM BY MR.
DUNHAM UNDER THE SPONSORSHIP OF THE DIVISION OF EDUCATION, 1956-7.

1. Wooden figure of a girl. H. 6⅞ in.
18th Dynasty. *Way Collection, 1872.*

I The Egyptian Collection, 1872-1905

THERE ARE several ways in which I might seek to familiarize the reader with our Egyptian Collection but I have chosen not simply to illustrate a series of the fine objects which are housed in the Department, but rather to relate the background of the formation of the collections, how they were acquired over many years and something of the considerable increase in our knowledge of Ancient Egypt which has come about as a result. In the course of my remarks we shall have occasion to consider a good many of our finest objects and in that way obtain an idea of the collection as a whole.

The Museum of Fine Arts is 88 years old, having been incorporated in 1870. At first a very modest enterprise it had no building of its own and in 1872 first began serving the Boston public by exhibiting paintings in two galleries in the Boston Athenaeum. Four years later, in 1876, the first wing of the Old Museum building on Copley Square, on the site of the present Sheraton-Plaza Hotel, was opened to the public and fourteen years later still, in 1890, that building was finally completed. The nucleus of the Egyptian collection was acquired by gift in 1872 when a Bostonian, the late C. Granville Way, presented the Museum with the residue of the collection formed by the Englishman, Robert Hay, a frequent visitor to Egypt between 1824 and 1838, who sold the bulk of his collection to the British Museum in 1865 and the remainder to Mr. Way's father. This collection formed during the third and fourth decades of the 19th century, was quite extensive and consisted mostly of many small objects. At that time the art of forgery was in its infancy, but while the great majority of pieces were genuine enough they had originally been acquired from dealers or peasants up and down the country and we are without any knowledge as to their place of origin. Now it is of great importance for us to know whenever possible the source from which an ancient Egyptian object comes, the provenance as we call it. Most objects coming from dealers cannot be traced to the original finding place and so we are often reduced to relying on guess-work as to their date and place in the archaeological picture and indeed as to their authenticity, for today the forger of antiquities is so unbelievably skillful and so well informed that even the best experts are not always immune to deception. The Way Collection, as I have said, contains many small objects, some of them rare and beautiful; among them are two little pieces which are particular favorites of mine: a charming little wooden statuette of a dancing girl, (fig. 1) dateable probably to the 18th Dynasty, and an unusual little stone tablet (fig. 2) bearing an unfinished sketch of the traditional subject, the king slaying foreign captives. Among the most popular exhibits given to the Museum by Mr. Way were a number of mummies, always appealing to small boys and still today perhaps the most frequently sought out objects in the Museum, especially by the younger generation.

Among the earliest acquisitions in the Egyptian field were several pieces of large sculpture which came to us in a way of special interest to Bostonians. Mr. John Lowell of Boston made an extensive and arduous journey in the eastern Mediterranean about 1835, including a trip through Egypt and up into the Sudan. At Luxor in Upper Egypt he bought a number of pieces of granite sculpture, most if not all, from the ruins of the great temple at Karnak. In Luxor he fell ill and made a will which contained a provision founding the Lowell Institute whose present head is today President of our Board of Trustees. He then resumed his travels southward crossing the Red Sea where he suffered shipwreck and eventually reached Bombay where he died. But the sculptures acquired by him in Luxor reached America safely, and in 1875 were presented to the Museum by his brother, Francis Cabot Lowell. They formed the second important accession to the young institution in the Egyptian field. Among these pieces were a colossal royal head, two fine fragments from the broken obelisk of Queen Hatshepsut (fig. 3) and a fine black granite statue of the lion-headed goddess, Sekhmet (fig. 4).

For ten years after 1875 the collection was increased by a number of gifts of small objects, amulets, scarabs, funerary figures, bronzes and the like, together with a number of paper squeezes made from the standing monuments in Egypt, some of which have now become quite valuable since the originals have deteriorated with the lapse of time. These additions were the result of the generosity of ten private donors. With the exception of the squeezes, however, they were of relatively minor importance for they came to us without any documentation as to source. During this period also the Museum acquired a good many casts of well-known Egyptian monuments, mostly in the Cairo Museum.

Then in 1885, a new approach was made by the Trustees to the problem of acquiring objects for the collection. Hitherto, the Museum had relied on gifts from individuals and this source continued to provide additions and does so, to some extent, even to the present time. Between 1885 and 1905, fifteen other individuals

2. Pinkish Limestone. Sketched scene.
H. 2½ in. New Kingdom.
Way Collection, 1872.

3. Red granite fragment from an
obelisk of Queen Hatshepsut.
H. 42 in. 18th Dynasty. From Karnak.
Gift of the heirs of Francis Cabot Lowell, 1875.

4. Black granite seated statue
of the goddess Sekhmet. H. 5 ft. 5½ in.
18th Dynasty. From Karnak.
*Gift of John A. Lowell
and Miss Lowell, 1875.*

made further gifts to the collection. The Egypt Exploration Fund, an English research society (later to become the Egypt Exploration Society), was carrying on archaeological excavations in Egypt financed by interested donors and by museums and universities in England. In return for their contributions the subscribers received a share of the objects found. This method of acquisition had two advantages. It tended to be less costly than purchasing on the market, because there was no profit to be considered, the Society working purely for the advancement of knowledge and in the most economical way, and it had the great merit that objects had a known provenance which was made available in the reports of its excavations published by the Society. From 1885 to 1905, the Trustees of the Museum subscribed regularly to the Egypt Exploration Society with the result that a substantial number of first-class objects from their excavations came to us nominally as gifts from the Society. I can only mention a few of these. Among them, from a site in Middle Egypt known as Hu, came a little marble head which at first was thought to be that of a Ptolemaic king (fig. 5), but in quite recent years the body which belongs to this head and which fits onto it, was discovered in the Louvre in Paris, bearing the cartouche of King Amenhotep II of the 18th Dynasty. From Nebesheh in the Delta comes a large granite statue of Ramesses II (fig. 7) and, made for the same king, from Heracleopolis, comes an architectural element in the form of a granite column with palm capital inscribed with the name of Ramesses. One of the most attractive objects which came to us from the Egypt Exploration Society during these years was a charming limestone relief from Nebesheh representing an unknown king of the Theban New Kingdom (fig. 6). Another statue, this time from Abydos, was the portrait in a seated position of a vizier of the 19th Dynasty whose name was Para-hotep. From the Fayum, that large oasis just west of the Nile in Lower Egypt, comes a mummy portrait of the Roman Period painted on wood (fig. 8).

Theodore M. Davis, a wealthy American from Newport with a keen interest in Egypt, obtained a concession from the Egyptian government to excavate in the Valley of the Kings at Thebes in the early years of the present century. With the assistance of trained scholars and at his own expense, he made a number of important discoveries, notably the tomb of King Tuthmosis IV of the 18th Dynasty which yielded significant additions to the Cairo Museum. As was the practice under permits granted by the Egyptian government, the excavator received a portion of the finds and Davis distributed these to the two major museums in his own country, the Metropolitan in New York and our own Museum. In this

5

5. Marble head of King Amenhotep II. H. 5 in.
18th Dynasty. From Hu.
Gift of Egypt Exploration Fund.

6. Limestone relief portrait of an unknown king.
H. 24½ in. New Kingdom. From Nebesheh.
Gift of Egypt Exploration Fund.

7. Black granite seated statue of Ramesses II.
H. 6 ft. 8¾ in. 19th Dynasty. From Nebesheh.
Gift of Egypt Exploration Fund.

8   9

10

11

8. Wooden panel: painted mummy portrait. H. 7½ in.
2nd Century A.D. From the Fayum. *Gift of Egypt Exploration Fund.*

9. Limestone head from a statuette. H. 2 in. 5th Dynasty. From Abydos.
Emily Esther Sears Fund (Purchased by Albert M. Lythgoe).

10. Wooden figure of a panther, coated with pitch. H. 13 in.
18th Dynasty. From Tomb of Tuthmosis IV at Thebes.
Gift of Theodore M. Davis.

11. Wooden panel from arm of a chair. H. 8⅞ in.
18th Dynasty. From tomb of Tuthmosis IV at Thebes.
Gift of Theodore M. Davis.

way we obtained by gift from Mr. Davis, a considerable group of the funerary equipment of Tuthmosis IV, among which I should mention the carved arm of a wooden chair with a scene of the king represented as a sphinx trampling upon his enemies (fig. 11), and a wooden figure of a panther covered with a bitumen-like black substance, of great spirit and beauty in spite of its somewhat fragmentary condition (fig. 10). We also obtained from him the important quartzite sarcophagus originally made for Queen Hatshepsut and then altered for the use of Tuthmosis I, and a remarkable garment made from gazelle skin which is an amazing example of the technical skill of Egyptian craftsmen.

Meanwhile the Museum was growing and expanding in its various fields and it was becoming obvious that the building in Copley Square would not long suffice for the housing of the collections, since enlarging of the building was impossible on the restricted site. With a view to future needs the Trustees, therefore, purchased in 1899 a plot of land in the Fenway abutting on Huntington Avenue and began planning for a new Museum building by appointing a Committee to study the best and latest in Museum designs both in this country and abroad. The resulting new building was started about five years later and was opened in 1909.

As the Museum grew and developed, its internal organization also became more complex. Varied collections, paintings, prints, sculpture and decorative arts, textiles, and the formation of outstanding collections of Egyptian and Far Eastern Art, meant a growing complexity with which no single head could hope to have the varied knowledge to cope. To the demands on the Director for administrative management of a vital and expanding institution were added the need for expert knowledge in many fields of connoisseurship. Thus it became inevitable that the Museum should be sub-divided into smaller units of more manageable size. The Director became primarily the administrative head of the Museum responsible directly to the Trustees, while under his general supervision there grew up departments, each confining its activities to its special field and in charge of a Curator who was appointed directly by the Board of Trustees, but who worked under the Director. The Curators took over the detailed management of their departments, the exhibition of the collections, recommendation of purchases and other acquisitions, the study of the objects in their charge, and the giving of information about them. The Director was thus assisted in his task by having the advice of a group of specialized experts, each representing a different department.

In 1902 the Trustees established the Department of Egyptian Art and named Albert M. Lythgoe as its first Curator. With funds provided by the Trustees, he now embarked on a number of purchases in Egypt, with one exception the first time that the Museum had undertaken to increase its Egyptian material by this method. (The one exception was the purchase in 1893 of another fine painted mummy portrait of Graeco-Roman date from the Fayum). Lythgoe went to Egypt partly to purchase antiquities for the Department and partly to gain experience in excavating by collaborating with Dr. George A. Reisner, who headed an expedition for the University of California financed by Mrs. Phoebe Hearst, mother of the well-known newspaper proprietor, William Randolph Hearst. Reisner was a graduate of Harvard, originally an Assyriologist, but who had studied in Germany under the great Egyptologists, Erman and Sethe, and was already recognized as the leading American excavator in Egypt at that time. I shall have more to say about Reisner later on; for the present I want only to mention some of the objects purchased for the Museum by Lythgoe in the years 1903 and 1904, pieces of known origin and of undoubted authenticity and hence of enhanced value to the Museum. These purchases ranged all the way from slate palettes of pre-dynastic date from Nagada to pieces of the New Kingdom, but here I can only mention three single objects. One is a small limestone head of very fine workmanship from Abydos dating to the 5th Dynasty (fig. 9). Another piece of great importance was a wooden statue from Assiut which came from the excavations of the Frenchman, Chassinat, and finally among our great treasures acquired at this period were a group of tiles representing foreign captives from the palace at Medinet Habu at Thebes and which date to the 19th Dynasty.

One other acquisition of major importance was made during this period not by Lythgoe, but by the late E. P. Warren, an expert primarily occupied with Classical antiquities, in which field he had made several important purchases for the Museum. This is a small green slate portrait head broken from a statuette, the date of which has been the subject of much discussion, but which we now think should be placed at or near the end of the dynastic period, corresponding to the Hellenistic Roman phase of Mediterranean culture and marked by a brutally realistic type of portraiture (fig. 12). I want to lay special emphasis on this little head because it is generally acknowledged to be one of our great treasures matched, though hardly surpassed, by only one other piece of like nature, the famous "green head" in Berlin.

Thus the period from 1872 to 1905, was one of formation and early growth through gifts and purchases, and the years when the limited gallery space afforded by the old building in Copley Square became filled to overflowing.

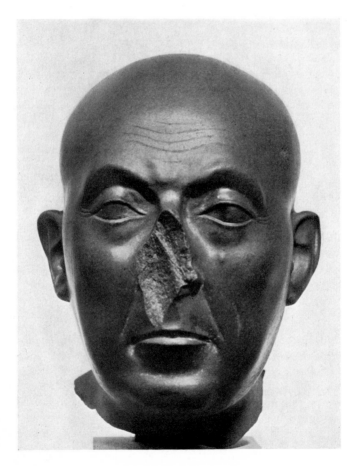

12. Slate portrait head. H. 4⅛ in. 26th-30th Dynasty?
Pierce Fund (Purchased by Edward P. Warren, 1904).

II The Department of Egyptian Art and The Harvard–Boston Expedition

THE YEAR 1905 brought with it changes both in the Museum and the Department: Edward M. Robinson relinquished the directorship to go to the Metropolitan in New York, taking with him the experience and many of the new ideas and techniques developed in Boston. In the same year Dr. Reisner's expedition in Egypt became affiliated with the Museum. It was, I believe, in 1904 that Mrs. Phoebe Hearst advised Reisner that she could no longer finance his work in Egypt on behalf of the University of California and he found himself faced with two alternatives: either to abandon his excavations and face the break-up of the organization which he had developed and the relinquishment of his concession at Giza hard by the Great Pyramid, or find other support and a new sponsor. At the time, Mr. Lythgoe, Curator of the Department, was working in Egypt, taking part in Reisner's excavations by way of gaining field experience, and purchasing for the Museum. He also held a lectureship at Harvard. Reisner was himself a Harvard man, obtained his Ph.D. there, had done graduate work in Germany, and had already made his mark as a brilliant and thorough scholar and an outstanding excavator. The Museum wanted to expand its Egyptian collection and was by this time cognizant of the desirability of obtaining works of art of known and documented origin and of unquestioned authenticity. Already Lythgoe had been emphasizing this scholarly approach in his purchases. All these considerations added up to an obvious answer. President Eliot of Harvard and Gardner Lane, President of the Trustees of the Museum, reached a gentlemen's agreement: Harvard saw advantage to the University in taking part in scientific excavations in the interest of scholarship and the advancement of learning; the Museum desired to add to its collection of authentic and documented works of art. Reisner himself was alive to the value of being associated with one of the world's greatest universities and one of America's leading museums, and with the assurance of adequate financial support for his work which would result. The Harvard University—Museum of Fine Arts Egyptian Expedition was set up with Reisner as Director of the Expedition and Lythgoe as Field Director. Reisner was thus enabled to continue his excavations at Giza without interruption and to keep his staff of trained Egyptian workmen together.

Presently I shall return to the subject of the Expedition which has been for many years of such vital importance to the growth and the quality of the Egyptian collection in Boston. But first let me give you a few historical facts. In 1906, Lythgoe after a year of work with Reisner in Egypt, resigned as Curator of the Department in order to accept a call to join Mr. Robinson at the Metropolitan as Curator of the Egyptian collection there and to initiate the Metropolitan Museum's own excavations in Egypt. In the same year Mr. Oric Bates was named Temporary Assistant in charge of the Department, but served only one year, resigning then for study abroad. In 1908, the Trustees appointed L. Earle Rowe to the same post of Temporary Assistant in Charge, but he too held the position for only about a year and later became Director of the Museum of the Rhode Island School of Design in Providence. Finally in 1910, Reisner, who remained for the most part in Egypt with only periodic and rather brief visits to Boston, was appointed Curator of Egyptian Art, the second to hold the position. Meanwhile the new Museum was rising on Huntington Avenue. In 1909 the entire collections from the Copley Square building were re-installed in more ample quarters, and the present Museum, or rather the nucleus of it, was opened for business. At that time the Egyptian Department had four galleries on the upper floor and two study rooms on the ground floor, together with a small office. Today it has seven galleries upstairs, four study rooms on the ground floor, plus an office, a Departmental library, and an archives room, which has recently been sub-divided by a partition for the greater convenience of visiting scholars working on our voluminous records. This does not include storage space in the basement, which has been greatly expanded.

Thus in the forty-nine years since we moved into the present building the space occupied by the Department has more than doubled, an indication of the growth in both its collections and its work, due almost entirely to its association with the Harvard University — Museum of Fine Arts Expedition. And this growth has also been reflected in personnel. From the inauguration of the Expedition in 1905 until 1928, the staff in Boston was somewhat sporadic in nature. Reisner spent most of his time in Egypt and was seldom here for long. I have mentioned Oric Bates and L. E. Rowe, both of whom were temporarily in charge for short periods. In 1914 I joined the Expedition and spent part of my time in Boston from then until 1928, mostly during summers between periods of field work in Egypt, and held the post of Assistant in the Department. During my absences, Mr. Ashton Sanborn, Secretary of the Museum, and Mr. H. Lyman Story, Registrar, did what had to be done in the Department in addition to their other duties. Mr. Sanborn had had field experience in Egypt with Reisner and others although he had been primarily trained as a Classical scholar, and Mr. Story had also worked for a short time with the Expedition. In 1928 I returned definitively from Egypt and took up permanent residence in Boston, being made successively Assistant Curator, Associate Curator, and after Reisner's death in 1942, Curator. I had to assist me Mr. William Stevenson Smith and Miss Suzanne Chapman. At the end of 1955 I resigned in order to devote all my time to the work of publishing the scientific reports on Reisner's work in the Sudan, much of which he had been unable to do before his death. My successor as Curator, the fourth in the line, is Dr. William Stevenson Smith who, like myself, had served for many years with Reisner in Egypt, and who is today acknowledged to be one of the leading scholars in the world in the field of Egyptian Art History.

In the following pages I shall be dealing almost exclusively with the work done by the Egyptian Expedition: with the magnificent series of works of art which have come to the Museum from it, and with the great contributions to knowledge which it has made over the years. The founder and Director of the Expedition, George A. Reisner, was a remarkable man and a great scholar. I knew him well, was trained by him, and worked under him throughout the later years of his career. He was a dedicated man devoted utterly to the service of scholarship, for which he made many sacrifices both of his own comfort and that of his family. He was largely indifferent to the amenities of life as he was to its financial rewards, and to him money was simply a necessary means to furthering the work of the Expedition. His natural bent as well as his thorough training in scholarly methods under the great German archaeologists in his early days, made him a leader in the application of scientific methods to excavating, and he trained many of the leading Egyptologists of recent years. At the start of his career as an excavator he began developing an organization of native Egyptian workmen and a method of keeping records which he gradually perfected until it became a model copied by others.

The process of excavating an ancient site is complex, but in its essentials it involves a sort of dissection — taking apart and separating out the component elements — buildings or the remains thereof, and the varied objects deposited in them or in the ground beneath them. This process means the destruction of the site, the destruction of the evidence in one sense, and it can only be justified if a complete and permanent record of every step in the process is made at the time.

Reisner used to say the records of a well conducted excavation should enable future scholars to reconstruct in every detail the conditions found by the excavator. This ideal, though seldom if ever completely attained, was at least approached in the records of our Expedition. These were essentially as follows: *first* came the Diary, which was written up every day by the head of the Expedition, and which recorded exactly what work was done on that day, by whom done, the conditions observed and the objects unearthed, and with comments on what, at that stage, appeared to be the significance of the work. This Diary often included sketches and measurements to help explain to others what was verbally described. *Second* came photography, done by specially trained Egyptians under the direction of the excavator. Every stage of the work, every object found, was visually recorded at the time, and as objects were removed from the ground they were again photographed, sometimes from several angles. *Third*, there was what was known as the Object Register. This was a large ledger, kept in duplicate, in which every single object or fragment — potsherds, beads, scraps of every kind as well as important objects — was entered with an identifying number, a careful verbal description, usually a measured drawing, measurements, date, place of finding, and a note of photographs taken. In addition to these day-by-day records, maps and plans of the site and of individual buildings had to be made, and the supervision and direction of the workmen had to be seen to. One can well imagine that when a large gang of men was excavating a rich site the recorders were kept pretty busy.

Reisner, in addition to developing this system of recording, built up an organization of specially trained Egyptian workmen whose skill and loyalty to the Expedition were remarkable. Flinders Petrie, the famed British excavator, who started digging in the 1880s, was the first to employ men from the village of Quft in Upper Egypt, and Reisner followed the same practice for he found that "Quftis" were already specialists at this work, in which they had been employed for a generation by the great British excavator. These men were all recruited from a limited group of families in that village so that most of them were related to each other, and their sense of clan or family solidarity made for a closely knit *esprit de corps* of great value. Reisner recruited them as mere boys who learned the business under older men of their families, and many of them developed into highly skilled specialists with really great knowledge of archaeology. In the course of the years, workmen trained by Reisner became the most sought after diggers for other expeditions and few have been without some key men trained by him.

13. Dr. George A. Reisner in his early 50s.

Reisner always gave first place to archaeology as a means toward the advancement of our knowledge of ancient Egyptian civilization, and often said that the acquisition of Museum objects was a by-product of his work — a necessary and desirable one because it was this by-product which obtained for him the financial support necessary to his work. That this by-product — works of art — was eminently worthwhile from the Museum point of view is, I think, obvious. It has meant that, because of Reisner's records, the magnificent collection which has come to us from the Expedition is of greatly increased value and usefulness because we know in detail all about its origin, its place in Egyptian culture, and the circumstances under which it was found, not to mention its unquestioned authenticity.

A good many years ago I made some calculations aimed at clarifying the monetary cost to the Museum of the collection — a calculation now much out of date. I took the total cost of running the Expedition from its first association with the Museum and placed against that the value for insurance in transit of the principal objects received during the same period, a valuation admittedly very low. The former was in round figures, about 10% of the latter. It is obvious, therefore, that from a purely dollars and cents point of view we have had a very good bargain. Clearly also, we have obtained through excavation masterpieces of Egyptian art which would simply not have been available for purchase at any price and on which it is really impossible to place any dollar valuation. Would anyone venture to name a price for the Hermes of Praxiteles? Then how arrive at the money value of such pieces as our Slate Pair of Mycerinus and his Queen, or the bust of Ankh-haf.

One might infer from the foregoing that the Museum has built up a collection at relatively little cost, and in a sense one would be right so far as actual cash outlay is concerned. However, there are other factors to be considered which are not always recognized. The excavator in Egypt has to work under a permit granted by the Egyptian Government, known as a concession. It is very exceptional for the government to grant a concession to an individual as such; the practice has been, and I presume still is, to allow excavation only by an experienced archaeologist working on behalf of a recognized scholarly organization such as a university of standing, a responsible museum, or such scientific organizations as the Egypt Exploration Society or the French Institute, and a few others. Once the government was satisfied on this score (it quite rightly sought to avoid irresponsible digging for private profit), it granted a concession under certain

14. Map of the Nile Valley, showing sites where the Museum's Expedition has worked.

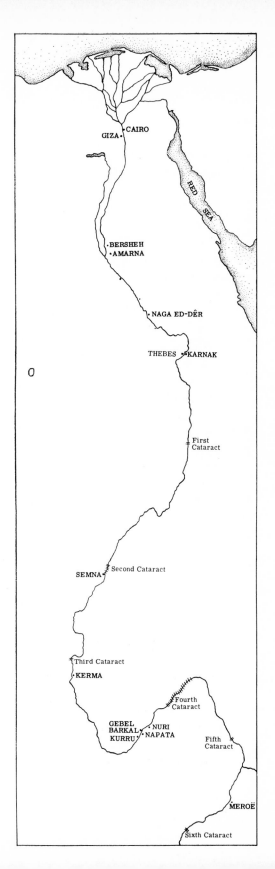

15. View of the West Cemetery at Giza, from top of the Great Pyramid.

conditions which were written into the contract made with the excavator as the representative of the sponsoring institution; in the case of Reisner, the Boston Museum and Harvard. Among these conditions were provisions as to the keeping of proper records, reporting all finds to the government, and acceptance of the obligation to publish scientific reports of the results within a reasonable time. In return for accepting these obligations the excavator was granted the right to dig in a specified area, to erect the necessary buildings on government land, and to obtain a share of the finds for his sponsoring institution. For over forty years Reisner worked in Egypt and the Sudan under contracts of this kind, first for the University of California and then for our Museum. In the beginning contracts provided for a division of the finds into two equal parts, one of which went to the excavator and the other to the Egyptian government. Later, with the rise of nationalist feeling among the Egyptians, the terms became less specific

16. View of the East Cemetery at Giza, from top of the Great Pyramid.

and more and more the finds assigned to the Expedition became uncertain.

Reisner was, I believe, remarkably successful in obtaining fair and even generous divisions from the government authorities, and this for two reasons. He knew Egypt and the Egyptian character intimately and enjoyed the respect and friendship of those with whom he had to deal, for he was himself always fair and straightforward in his dealings with them. Secondly, he lived in Egypt the year round and did not, like most excavators, return home at the end of each season. This meant that he did not have to divide his finds at the end of each dig, but could choose the strategic moment. It often happened that the yield of a season's work might contain only one outstanding object, such for example, as the portrait bust of Ankh-haf. If a division were to be made at such a time, the government would be sure to take the prize piece. By waiting until he had accumulated enough fine objects after another season or two, he could then ask for a division

17. The Third Pyramid and Funerary Temple of King Mycerinus at Giza.

18. View of the cliffs at El Bersheh, showing site of
the rock-cut tombs of the Middle Kingdom.

17

18

with the assurance of getting a part at least, of the best pieces. Actually this is how we obtained the bust I have just mentioned. It was the one important move-able find of the season, but Reisner held it in his storeroom for two or three years until he had found the tomb of Queen Hetep-heres. This unique group of royal tomb furniture of the Fourth Dynasty had to be kept in Cairo because it was from an undisturbed royal tomb which, by a special clause in the contract, must remain intact and in Egypt. The excavation of this sensational tomb occupied the en-tire time of the Expedition for nearly two years, and Reisner was able to make a successful plea for the bust for Boston as a make-weight against this find.

On the whole the Expedition received the benefits envisaged in its conces-sions, and on its side fulfilled its obligations to the Government. However, as time went on, the obligation to publish began to fall into arrears. Almost con-tinuous excavation for many years with limited funds and usually with inade-quate staff, and, in the later years, with Reisner's failing health and eye-sight, made this inevitable. To be sure, he published a number of monumental works and a host of short preliminary reports in the *Museum Bulletin* and elsewhere in scholarly journals, but despite his valiant efforts and his insatiable appetite for work, which lasted to the end of his life, the Expedition and the Museum found themselves at his death, faced with a mass of unpublished material with which he had been unable to deal. Reisner himself, as his health began to trouble him almost ten years before his death, realized the impossibility of completing this work, and in 1933 asked me to take over responsibility for publishing his ex-cavations in the Sudan, so that he might devote his remaining strength to the completion of his great work on the Giza excavations. Even this he was unable to do, and that work now rests on the shoulders of my colleague, Dr. Smith. Both of us were long associated with Reisner and feel ourselves in a very real sense to have inherited his obligations, and these obligations rest on us not only as his scholarly successors but also as representatives of the Museum, his sponsor-ing organization. It was primarily for this reason that I felt it necessary in 1955 to ask the Trustees to relieve me of the duties of the Curatorship so that I might devote myself to the completion of the major task of publishing the reports of the Expedition's work in the Sudan, where I had worked with Reisner. Thus, in my view, the magnificent collection which we owe so largely to Reisner and his Expedition has not been fully paid for as long as the excavation reports which the Museum owes, not only to the Egyptian and Sudan Governments, but to international scholarship, remain unpublished.

In the ensuing chapters, I propose to deal with the results of the Expedition's work as exhibited in our galleries, insofar as I can, with an account of their significance and the circumstances of their discovery. By consulting a map, one may gain some idea of the wide range and variety of Reisner's excavating activities, which began at the Giza Pyramid Plateau west of Cairo (fig. 14). Here were the headquarters of the Expedition and here Reisner worked almost continuously for nearly forty years. He excavated the major part of the great cemetery of mastaba tombs west of the Great Pyramid (fig. 15), the burial place of nobles and officials from the reign of Cheops into the Sixth Dynasty. He cleared the royal cemetery east of the Great Pyramid (fig. 16) containing the tombs of the mother of Cheops, his queens, his sons and daughters and their descendants. And he excavated the Pyramid and Valley Temples of King Mycerinus, builder of the Third Pyramid (fig. 17) and the three small pyramids of his queens. A little further south he excavated the Third Dynasty pyramid at Zawiyet-el-Ayran and adjacent tombs of that period and of the New Kingdom. Further south on the east bank of the Nile, he found at Bersheh (fig. 18) the finest painted wooden coffin of the Middle Kingdom ever to have come out of Egypt, and still further up the river in the cemeteries opposite the modern town of Girga, he dug a whole series of sites ranging in date from Pre-Dynastic to Middle Kingdom times. His work at Deir-el-Balas, north of Luxor, was done in his early years of excavating for the University of California, and his Survey of Lower Nubia was undertaken for the Egyptian Government, not for us.

Then in 1913 he began his great pioneering campaign in the Sudan which lasted until 1932, and which opened up a whole new chapter by revealing much of the ancient history of the land of Kush, Egypt's southern neighbor. As one continues up the Nile one passes the five Egyptian forts which he examined in the Second Cataract region and comes to the great Middle Kingdom site of Kerma above the Third Cataract, which revealed to the archaeologists an entirely unsuspected culture. Still further upstream, below the Fourth Cataract, is the great temple of Barkal which Reisner excavated together with the neighboring Kushite royal cemeteries of Kurru and Nuri, where he discovered the pyramid tombs of the Kushite 25th Dynasty of Egypt and those of their successors. Finally, between the Fifth Cataract and Khartoum, the Expedition excavated the three great cemeteries at Meroë which range from the 26th Dynasty down to the end of the Meroitic period in the middle of the fourth century A.D.

19. Alabaster seated statue of King Mycerinus. H. 7 ft. 8½ in.
4th Dynasty. From the Pyramid Temple of Mycerinus. *Expedition.*

III Old Kingdom Sculpture

THE Expedition worked on the great cemetery complex connected with the three pyramids of Giza from 1905 to the beginning of World War II. The portions of this vast site excavated by us were: *first*, the major part of the cemetery lying west of the Great Pyramid in which were buried the great nobles and court officials of the 4th to 6th Dynasties (see fig. 15); *second*, the Royal Cemetery which lay east and south-east of the Great Pyramid (see fig. 16), containing three small pyramids of the Queens of Cheops and the tombs of the royal sons and daughters and their descendants of the 4th and 5th Dynasties; *third*, the funerary complex of the third pyramid of King Mycerinus (see fig. 17), consisting of its Pyramid Temple against the east face of the pyramid, and the Valley Temple at the lower end of its causeway in the valley to the east, as well as the chapels and burial chambers of three small pyramids of the Queens of Mycerinus.

The colossal alabaster seated statue of King Mycerinus, which now faces the visitor when he enters the first Egyptian gallery in the Museum (fig. 19), once stood in the Pyramid Temple of Mycerinus. It had been broken up in ancient times, probably by seekers after treasure. The head and a large shoulder fragment were found outside the temple to the north, lying only a few inches below the surface, where it might have been discovered anytime during past centuries but, fortunately for us, never was. The large fragment of the knees, hands and legs, lay in one of the corridors of the Pyramid Temple, and other smaller fragments had been dispersed elsewhere in the neighborhood. When first shown in the Museum no attempt was made at restoration: the two main fragments, head and knees, were simply set up separately but in proper relation to each other. This arrangement, which had been dictated by a rather conservative dislike for restoring fine sculpture, hardly did justice to the quality of the figure, and some years later the left upper arm and shoulder, a large section of the torso, and the right foot, all of which had been found, were added, and an attempt at restoration of the missing parts was made. Whatever imperfections this restored figure may have, and the restorations can very easily be distinguished from the original parts, it at least gives some impression of the majesty of this colossal, kingly statue.

In the Valley Temple at the foot of the great causeway we found more examples of 4th Dynasty royal sculpture. Four alabaster seated statues of the king,
similar to, but somewhat smaller than, the figure I have just described, once
stood in the main courtyard. They were found grievously shattered though one,
which could be largely restored, is now with its head in the Cairo Museum, and
the fine head of a second, with pleated headdress, is also in Cairo together with
two shattered bases. Of the fourth seated statue only the lower part, up to the
waist of the figure, remained, but this was brought to Boston for its base was
beautifully ornamented with heraldic devices in sunk relief, originally filled with
blue color (fig. 20 a,b). Both sides of the seat bear designs combining hieroglyphic writing with symbolic representations. At the top two hawks, symbols of
the god Horus, hover protectively above two of the king's five names. Between
these on the right a lily supports the vulture *Nekhbet* of Upper Egypt, while below two seated figures representing the Nile hold the two plants which sym-
bolize Upper and Lower Egypt entwined about the hieroglyph which stands for
unity. On the other side of the throne a similar design appears, but this time
with the serpent, *Wadjet* of Lower Egypt, in the central position. On the back
of the throne a simpler design gives the Horus name of the king above the inter-
twined plants of the two kingdoms. These beautiful designs thus represent the
unity of the two lands, Upper and Lower Egypt, under the king, himself protected by the god Horus with whom he will become merged in the after-life.

In contrast to these large alabaster statues, is a tiny figure of Mycerinus in
ivory which was also found in the Valley Temple. It has neither head, arms,
nor feet, and only one leg, but it is of superlative modelling and is inscribed
with the king's name on the front of the belt. This little figure is exceptional
in that it represents the king in action. The body is slightly twisted and one
shoulder is raised a little, as if the left arm had been uplifted and the right arm
thrust forward.

The most impressive of all the statues found in the Valley Temple is undoubtedly the Slate Pair statue of Mycerinus and his Queen (fig. 21) which was
found practically intact at the bottom of a hole made by thieves. It is about
three-quarters life-size and shows the King standing with one leg advanced,
while the Queen stands at his left with one arm about his body. The two faces
are beautifully modelled and seem to have been finished, for the King's face
still shows traces of the red color with which it had been painted. But the group

20 a. Alabaster seat of a statue of
King Mycerinus. H. 3 ft. 2½ in. 4th Dynasty.
From Valley Temple of Mycerinus. *Expedition.*

20 b. The other side of above.

20 a

20 b

21. Slate group statue of Mycerinus and his Queen. H. 4 ft. 7 in.
4th Dynasty. From Valley Temple of Mycerinus. *Expedition.*

22. Slate group: Mycerinus, Hathor, and the Hare Nome. H. 2 ft. 9 in.
4th Dynasty. From Valley Temple of Mycerinus. *Expedition.*

22

as a whole was unfinished, the lower parts not having received their final smoothing, and tool marks may still be seen on the stone. No inscription giving the names of the King and Queen had been added, which would certainly have been the case had the work been completed.

Hard by, in the same part of the temple, the excavators came upon four remarkable triple groups in slate, all of them in a perfect state of preservation even to traces of the original coloring. Three of these groups consist of three standing figures against a slab, showing the king wearing the white crown of Upper Egypt in the center, with the goddess Hathor at his right and another standing figure at his left, the latter representing in each case, the personification of one of the provinces or "Nomes" of Upper Egypt. The three represented are the fourth (Thebes), the seventh (Diospolis Parva) and the seventeenth (Cynopolis). These are now in the Cairo Museum. The fourth, which is in Boston, is somewhat different in grouping (fig. 22): in the center is a seated figure of the goddess Hathor embracing on her left a standing figure of King Mycerinus, while on the other side stands the female personification of the fifteenth Upper Egyptian Nome (Hermopolis) whose symbol, a hare, rises above her head.

One more outstanding piece of royal sculpture was found in the Valley Temple. This was a beautiful youthful head in translucent alabaster, wearing what appears to be a close-fitting cap or head-cloth, and with the beard and the uraeus-serpent on its brow which mark it as a king. It is without inscription and has been thought possibly to be a portrait of Shepseskaf, the successor of Mycerinus, who is known to have finished the temple after his father's death. Others have considered it to be a portrait of Mycerinus himself, made when he was young. However this may be, it is a delicate and beautiful example of the best in royal sculpture of the Fourth Dynasty and one of the great treasures of our Museum (fig. 23).

The royal sculptures from the Mycerinus temples described above form but a small part of the treasures recovered from our excavations at Giza. There were in addition, a number of portraits of members of the royal family of the Fourth Dynasty of which I shall have time to mention only three here, all of them in our great First Gallery in Boston. The first of these is a little statuette of the eldest son of Mycerinus, Prince Khunera (fig. 24), who is represented seated cross-legged in the traditional attitude of a scribe or educated man who could read and write, a rare accomplishment at this early date. The figure is made of fine yellow limestone and is complete except for the hands and one foot. The face is perfect and most beautifully modelled. The hands once rested on the lap where one imagines a roll of papyrus spread out, on which the prince was about to write. The statuette is uninscribed, but was found in the prince's tomb just south of the Third Pyramid and is undoubtedly his portrait. Another statuette in the same material was found in the royal cemetery east of the Great Pyramid. It had unfortunately been broken into a number of pieces and some parts are missing, but it was originally of very fine quality and is of special importance because it is a unique group of two ladies in a pose not previously known (fig. 25). An inscription on the base tells us that the ladies are Queen Hetep-heres II and her daughter, Queen Meresankh III. Now our Expedition has excavated the tombs of both these ladies and from preserved inscriptions we know more or less about them. Queen Hetep-heres II was the daughter of Cheops, builder of the Great Pyramid. She had successively two husbands who were her own brothers or half-brothers, for both were sons of Cheops. Such marriages seem rather shocking to us but among the royalties of ancient Egypt they were looked upon with favor for they tended to ensure the purity of the divine royal blood. Her first husband was Cheops' eldest son, Prince Ka-waab, and he was the father of Meresankh III. He seems to have died before succeeding to the throne and Hetep-heres then married King Radedef, successor to Cheops, thus acquiring the title of queen. After a short and stormy reign he too died, or was murdered by his brother Chephren, builder of the Second Giza Pyramid. Her daughter, Meresankh III, being of the blood royal, was married to another king, probably Chephren, though we are not certain, and he may have been Mycerinus. The fragments of this remarkable statuette have been put together and the missing parts have been restored in plaster. Hetep-heres stands on the left with her left arm thrown over the shoulder and around the neck of her daughter in an appealingly protective pose.

Prince Ankh-haf, a son of Sneferu by a minor queen, has left us what is undoubtedly the most realistic surviving portrait of an Egyptian royal prince of the pyramid age. This is a painted limestone bust (fig. 26), found by us lying overthrown in the remains of the mud-brick chapel of his tomb. The nose is broken, the ears are missing, and there is a large bruise on the forehead, but despite these injuries the face impresses one as an unquestionably faithful likeness of a powerful and intelligent man who, though he lived nearly five thousand years ago, seems to live again in this portrait. The nose is slightly aquiline, the lips are full but firm and the eyes with pronounced pouches under them,

42

23. Alabaster Royal Head,
perhaps the young Mycerinus?
H. 11¼ in. 4th Dynasty. From Giza. *Expedition.*

24. Yellow limestone statuette
of Prince Khunera as a scribe.
H. 12 in. 4th Dynasty. From Giza. *Expedition.*

23   24

25. Yellow limestone group statuette
of Queen Hetep-heres II
and her daughter Meresankh III (restored).
H. 1 ft. 11¾ in. 4th Dynasty. From Giza. *Expedition.*

are small, close set, and completely realistic in modelling. In every feature the face bespeaks strength, authority, and the consciousness of power as befits the first minister of the kingdom and the heir to the throne.

Among the most beautiful and important finds at Giza was a series of portrait heads of great nobles and ladies of the 4th Dynasty which were found in the burial pits of the great mastaba-tombs in the Western Cemetery. Five of these now stand in individual cases in our first Egyptian gallery. They are known to Egyptologists as "reserve heads" and only a dozen or so have ever been found. They form a unique class of Egyptian sculpture and are confined in date to the 4th and 5th Dynasty and in provenance to Giza and Saqqara. These heads are of unpainted white limestone and were never parts of statues, and they all come from the burial pits of important tombs. The purpose for which they are thought to have been made is interesting. In these relatively early days the art of mummification had not reached the perfection which it attained in the New Kingdom, and people must have become aware that the preservation of the dead in the likeness of the living man, so important in Egyptian minds to the welfare of the spirit in the after-life, was not being satisfactorily attained. They went to considerable lengths in their attempt to retain the likeness to the living, as for instance, when we find the face modelled in plaster over the wrappings of Old Kingdom mummies. These "reserve heads" were one form of this attempt: they were thought of as substitutes for the actual head and face, to take its place for the use of the spirit, should the resemblance of the latter to the living man cease to be satisfactory. All have been found either in the burial chambers themselves or immediately outside them where they were probably thrown by ancient tomb robbers who were not interested in works of art, but only in things of value such as gold, jewelry and the like. By their very purpose these heads are intended to be true portraits, and a glance at the five on display shows that each is distinctive and different from all the others. The head of a Treasury official named Nofer (fig. 27a), has a markedly aquiline nose and distinctive contours of lips and throat, which, seen in profile, are faithfully depicted in the relief portrait of the same man seen near by. We can name only one of the other four heads in the gallery, that of a Princess Merytyetes, whose features are quite characteristic of the Egyptian type of beauty. Not so the face of a nameless lady opposite, whose up-tilted nose gives her a distinctly piquant air (fig. 27b). Highly contrasted with each other, as with the rest of our reserve heads, are the features of the nameless princely couple who face each other further on. The woman is heavy featured and strongly suggests the negro (fig. 27d), while her husband (fig. 27c) has a narrow thin face and a distinctly sour expression. Both come from the same tomb, and one cannot help speculating whether they may not be the partners in an ancient diplomatic alliance, in which a prince of the Egyptian royal family was married to the daughter of an African chieftain for reasons of state.

Most of the sculpture which has survived from the Old Kingdom is of stone, but in fact we know that a large number of statues and statuettes were made of wood. These are, naturally, but seldom preserved, and we count ourselves particularly fortunate in having found one of these at Giza which is among the finest that have survived (fig. 28). It dates from the 6th Dynasty, near the end of the period when the West Cemetery was in use and belonged to a member of a family of royal architects and builders named Mehy. It was found lying on its right side which has consequently suffered severely from decay, but the left side of the face is fortunately in perfect condition, and only the eyes, which had been set in bronze rims, are lost. The figure is somewhat smaller than life and is depicted striding forward with the left hand advanced to grasp a staff. Although no trace remains of the original coloring, the modelling of the face is sensitive and the workmanship is of the best.

The excavations at Giza yielded many statues and statuettes of which a goodly number are represented in the Museum. It is clear that every tomb of a well-to-do Egyptian of the Old Kingdom had one or more figures of the owner and often of members of his family and even servants as well. Usually these were walled up in a closed chamber and were not intended to be seen. Their function according to Egyptian beliefs was to serve as substitute bodies for the dead — images of him to which the spirit might return at will for renewal in the after-life and to partake of the offerings of food and drink made periodically in the tomb chapel by the mortuary priests, whose duty it was to keep the dead supplied. This function is made evident by the fact that the statue chamber was usually placed directly behind the offering place in the chapel, and indeed sometimes had a little opening communicating with it through which the aroma of the offerings and the words of the incantations were wafted to the statue behind. In the tombs of wealthy and important people the statues were sometimes beautifully made, as for instance in the tomb of a high official named Pen-Meruw, who is depicted standing in a niche accompanied by his wife and children, and depicted in duplicate, once for each of the two principal offices which he held.

a   b

On the other hand, even rather poor people strove to supply their tombs with a statue and we have one example of such a figure from a quite insignificant little tomb, where it is obvious that the owner could not afford to employ a skillful sculptor but had to rely on the services of some rather incompetent stone-cutter to supply his need.

The walls of the tomb chapels at Giza were often embellished with reliefs and inscriptions from which we have obtained not only much information about their owners and the mortuary ritual practised, but also much about the daily life of the Egyptians of the Old Kingdom. It should be realized that both the inscriptions and the pictured scenes were put there not primarily as decoration but for the benefit of the spirits of the dead who inhabited the tombs. For the Egyptians believed that the scenes would become reality and the inscribed words turn into facts in the after-life. Thus, the owner pictured seated at a table before piles of good things to eat might enjoy in perpetuity the feast set out on the wall or, in another well-known scene, might forever sit with his wife playing games of draughts. To our modern western eyes these pictures are often a little difficult to interpret, for they are drawn in a convention unfamiliar to us. The essential point to be grasped in looking at Egyptian two-dimensional representation is this: it does not seek to show what our eyes would see at any one time or from any given point, but rather to explain to the observer what is there — what the artist wants to tell him. In order to accomplish this there is no hesitation in com-

 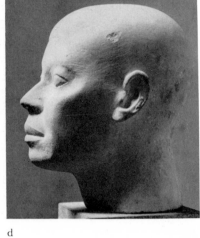

c   d

27 a, b, c, d.
Four limestone "Reserve Heads".
Life size. 4th Dynasty.
From Mastaba tombs at Giza. *Expedition.*

28. Wooden statue of the architect Mehy.
H. 3 ft. 5¾ in. 5th Dynasty.
From Giza. *Expedition.*

28

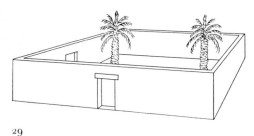

29. Hypothetical Scene:
a walled garden drawn in perspective.

30. The same scene as fig. 29
as it would have been represented
by an ancient Egyptian.

29

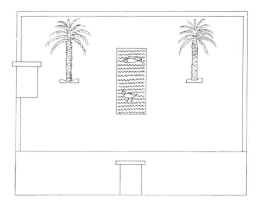

31. Outline drawing of a boating scene
from the tomb of Queen Meresankh III
at Giza.

32. The same scene as fig. 31
"translated" into Western perspective.

30

bining in a single scene several aspects, or even to represent things which were
not visible at all. The usual drawing of the human figure shows this principle
well: the head is depicted in profile so that the contours of nose, mouth and
chin may be seen to best advantage. But the eye is placed in this head as if seen
from in front, because from that aspect the shape of the eye is more characteristic than when seen from the side. The important thing about shoulders is that
they project on either side below the neck, and so in order that this may be evident they are drawn as if seen from in front. But despite this, in figures of women
the breast is shown in side view in order that its contour may be apparent, and
only one is drawn. To us such drawing may seem childish, but it was accepted
by the Egyptians as normal, perhaps partly because they had a simple almost
childlike approach in the remote period when their conventions began to take
shape, and these, once established, were found satisfactory and became a matter
of habit.

In some ways I believe this method of drawing has advantages over our own convention of representing what may be seen from a single viewpoint. To illustrate this let us take a hypothetical scene. Let us imagine a walled enclosure of rectangular shape with doorways in the center of two adjoining sides. Inside this enclosure let us place two palm trees, each having its base surrounded by a little dike of mud to retain the water with which the tree is irrigated. In the center of the enclosure is a pool of water in which a fish is swimming and on the surface of which rests a duck. These are the facts we want to represent. I have attempted to draw this imaginery scene from one point of view as we might (fig. 29), and again as the Egyptians would have done (fig. 30). Our western version may look like what we would see, but it does not begin to tell us the facts half as well as the Egyptian version, even though the latter looks like nothing we could actually view.

Now let us take an actual scene found on one of the walls of the tomb of that same Queen Meresankh III, whose statue in the company of her mother, Hetep-heres II, we saw earlier. The scene is a charming one in which Hetep-heres and Meresankh, accompanied by a small boy, are standing on a boat at the edge of a papyrus thicket, engaged in plucking stalks of the plant, while a boatman in the stern steadies the craft with a pole. The scene is somewhat damaged and not easily distinguishable in a photograph, so I have had it faithfully copied in outline (fig. 31). One notices at once that the ladies are so large that the boat could not possibly have stayed afloat, and both the child and the boatman are too small in proportion to the ladies. That is, of course, a way of indicating which of the figures were important and which merely incidental. On the right the papyrus thicket is so conventionalized as to be hard to identify unless one were familiar with such subjects and in the same way the water below is represented by a series of regular wavy lines. Now what the artist had in mind was clear enough, but we should draw it in quite a different way as Miss Suzanne Chapman has done in this reconstruction in modern western perspective (fig. 32).

IV The Tomb of Queen Hetep-heres

THE GENERAL PUBLIC is apt to think of archaeological excavation as being a very romantic and exciting occupation. In sober fact it is far more frequently a matter of patience, hard work, and much disappointment. Only after months and sometimes years of labor, first in the field and later in working over the records, do results become evident and add, if we are fortunate, to our growing body of knowledge. Now and then, at rather rare intervals, spectacular "finds" do turn up to act as stimulants and give encouragement to those engaged in the laborious routine of note-taking, drawing, measuring and photographing. Such a one we had the good fortune to make at Giza in 1925.

The Expedition had been systematically clearing the great Royal Cemetery at Giza which lies immediately east of the Great Pyramid. Here, south-east of the site where once stood the funerary temple of Cheops, lie the three small pyramids of his queens, their eastern sides, with their small funerary chapels, facing on a street beyond which lie the tombs of Cheops' sons and daughters. One day the Expedition photographer was taking pictures at the northern end of this street, and in setting up his tripod on the rock surface, one of the legs sank into a soft spot. He investigated and discovered that there was a patch of plaster on the surface of the rock running north and south. When this had been photographed and removed, there appeared a trench filled with blocks of dressed limestone which sealed a stairway running down to the south and ending in a short tunnel. At the end of this tunnel the diggers came upon a mass of limestone blocks set in plaster and running both up and down. At this point the excavators paused and began to examine the surface of the street above. Careful sweeping of the rock presently revealed the outline of a square hole cunningly filled with large stones, the surfaces of which had been left rough so as to blend with the adjacent rock and effectively mask the mouth of a pit. Now burial shafts were well known at Giza, but they all went down through a tomb superstructure. This one had no superstructure and had been most carefully concealed by its makers. This secret pit, beneath the masking stones at the surface, was filled with squared limestone blocks set in plaster and quite undisturbed. Whatever it concealed had evidently never been tampered with, and our hopes rose at the thought. There followed weeks of patient work while layer after layer of the filling blocks were hoisted out of the ever deepening pit. Presently the entrance to the tunnel was exposed and passed and the pit continued down, roughly cut in the living rock but rectangular and fairly regular in form. Then an opening in the west wall of the pit came to light, carefully sealed with more limestone blocks. Excavation of the pit was suspended while this blocking was removed, exposing a small cavity or niche in which were found bones of an ox and several jars which had once contained beer. This was a food-offering made for the dead at the time of burial, quite undisturbed. The main pit went on down, still filled with blocks and plaster, and excavating continued. Fifty feet, seventy-five feet — the filling was rough and careless now, and among the limestone blocks were broken fragments of pottery basins which had been used for bringing down the plaster poured over the blocking stones. Finally at ninety feet down the filling began to be more careful. The blocks were neatly laid in rows and layers, set carefully in plaster. We knew that we must be getting near the bottom. On March 8, 1925, a block on the south edge of the pit was removed and behind it appeared a black hole. We had reached the burial chamber. More stones were taken out to enlarge the hole, flash-lights were brought, and we lay down and peered through the opening (fig. 33).

As the beams of the flash-light penetrated the gloom we could make out a small room cut out of the rock, about fifteen feet long and eight feet wide and approximately six feet high. The north-east quarter was filled with a plain alabaster sarcophagus, its lid still in place, and resting on it a mass of gold tubes, somewhat longer than the lid, and apparently hollow. Beside them on the lid, lay the decayed remains of some ornamented object, on which hieroglyphs could be made out, including a cartouche or royal oval with the name of Sneferu, father of Cheops. On the floor, to the west of the sarcophagus, lay a jumbled mass which was quite confusing, but we could make out a copper ewer and basin, a group of small alabaster vases, sheets of gold, and various golden bars which looked like parts of furniture. These lay among a mass of thin gold strips and bits of blue and green faience, together with two palm capitals in gold (fig. 34). At the far end of the little room appeared a piled mass of pottery in utter confusion, and on top of one large bowl, a golden lion's leg from a piece of furniture, upside down. There was not a square inch of unencumbered floor-space anywhere in the chamber. High up in the west wall a long opening was blocked with stones smeared over with plaster, masking a cavity in the rock. Now a great many burial chambers at Giza had been examined by the Expedition, all of them more or less plundered, but nevertheless showing us what was the normal ar-

33. Tomb chamber of Queen Hetep-heres I when first opened:
after a painting made on the site by the late Joseph Lindon Smith.

34. The deposit on the tomb of Hetep-heres.
Back part of chamber.

33

34

rangement. Generally the sarcophagus stood at the far end, and in this at the funeral, the dead had first been placed and the lid closed. Next to this the more valuable articles of furniture and personal equipment would be stacked, and last would be put the pottery and stone vessels to meet the cooking and eating requirements of the dead, and the containers of food and drink to supply him with food in the hereafter. The arrangement of the contents of this chamber were the reverse of normal: first to be deposited were the stone and pottery vessels, next the furniture and personal toilet requirements of the owner, and lastly the great sarcophagus slid in close to the doorway, and on top of it were laid the golden tubes and the inscribed object. This was entirely abnormal and puzzling, yet it was obvious that there had been no tampering with the contents after it had been placed there nearly 5000 years ago. It was also clear from the cartouche, which could be read, that the tomb had belonged to an important person having some association with the predecessor of Cheops, and the importance of the owner was further indicated by the large amount of gold visible in the tomb.

The clearing of this remarkable chamber of its contents took the Expedition the greater part of two seasons, and the subsequent study and reconstruction of its treasures occupied our attention for many years more. Indeed, it was not until 1955 that the final publication of the results was issued by the Harvard University Press. The difficulties entailed were formidable. The tiny chamber lay 100 feet down at the base of a vertical shaft, and lighting had to be devised so that we could see to work and to take the many photographs during the progress of the work, so that the record might be adequate. And the deposit in the chamber lay so thickly everywhere that it was impossible to enter without stepping on something. Originally, the space beside the sarcophagus had been filled with various pieces of wooden furniture cased in gold sheets and largely covered with ornaments consisting of colored faience inlays set in thin sheet gold. The wood of this furniture had completely decayed, leaving the gold sheets and the inlays scattered about in apparent confusion, yet the position of every piece in its relation to others had to be noted and recorded in full detail if we were ever to hope to be able to reconstruct the conditions which had prevailed when the deposit was made. Remember that in the beginning we did not know what to expect. No furniture of the Old Kingdom had ever been found up to this time — we did not know what it would look like, how it had been constructed, nor what the decoration of it would be like. It was thus essential that the record of our work should be as perfect as was humanly possible — no pains or time must be spared and every minutest point should be observed, noted and photographed. Our ideal was to make the record such that it would later be possible, in theory at least, to put everything back again exactly as we had found it, even to the minutest scrap of gold or faience inlay piece.

The method adopted was this. Starting at the base of the shaft and looking down on the first square foot of floor space, we made a plan of that area at full size, drawing in every object that could be seen as it lay. To check this we then took a vertical photograph of the same area, being careful to touch nothing. Then with drawing and photograph in hand, we started picking up the objects that had been so recorded, giving each an identifying number as we removed it, and marking this number on the plan. When everything visible on the plan had been removed, other things below became visible, and so the whole process was repeated, and we went down through the second layer in the same way, and so on, until we reached the rock floor of the chamber. In this way we cleared a space next the entrance and were able to advance into the tomb sufficiently to take up a further area in the same way. All the time we were studying the deposit, discussing the details and trying to determine the relation of one scrap to another, constantly making notes of our observations and theories, sometimes only to discard them the next day when further evidence showed them to be wrong, but always putting everything in writing, taking photographs, drawing detailed plans, and giving identifying numbers to everything picked up. In the end, after two long seasons of subterranean labor, we had 1700 photographs and something like 1500 pages of notes and plans as a permanent record of the work. Often we spent long hours discussing what lay before us without touching anything, trying to understand the meaning of how this piece came to lie in a certain position, and what its original relation to that other piece may have been. Often we worked delicately with tweezers, trying to lift one tiny inlay without disturbing others adjacent to it, and laying the group out on trays in their original order, so that we might thus reconstruct the designs which they had once formed. It was hot and stuffy down there, and we had to install a ventilation system with an electric fan, for the great 1000 candlepower lamps which lit our work generated heat as well as light. At first we squatted down in the confined space to work, but as we progressed into the chamber we lay on mattresses or sat on wooden boxes and eventually we were able to move in a small table and chair so as to work in greater comfort.

At first it was quite impossible to identify individual pieces of furniture, but gradually certain pieces began to become apparent even though their parts were disjointed and fallen out of place. The first piece of furniture to be recognized was the carrying chair. Its main frame had been sheathed in heavy sheet gold, and the pieces which composed it, ornamented with a mat pattern, had retained their shape and, of course, their original dimensions, for gold is one of the few materials which does not alter with the passage of time. In this case we were fortunate in finding still intact inside the gold sheathing some of the original wood which, although greatly shrunken and warped, enabled us to study and recover in detail the method used in making the joints of the carrying chair. This piece, too, enabled us for the first time to identify the owner of this secret tomb, for inlaid into strips of ebony let into its back, were little gold hieroglyphs which formed an inscription, repeated in four different places. Although the ebony strips were no longer preserved, the gold hieroglyphs lay approximately in their original arrangement and we were able to read the inscription (fig. 35). It said "Mother of the King of Upper and Lower Egypt, Follower of Horus, Guide of the Ruler, Favorite one, she whose every word is done for her, the Daughter of the God's body, Hetep-heres". Thus was the owner identified as a King's mother, a King's chief wife (the titles Follower of Horus, and Guide of the Ruler), and the daughter of a deceased King (Daughter of the God's body). So we found out that Hetep-heres, Queen of Sneferu (whose name we had already found) and daughter of a former king (probably Huni, the predecessor of Sneferu), was the mother of the king who had presented her with the carrying-chair (fig. 36), undoubtedly Cheops himself.

The second piece of furniture which was identified and reconstructed was the queen's bed, which had been laid in the tomb upside-down on top of other things. It too was sheathed in gold, but the center part was a wooden framework let in to the structure, and most probably supporting a laced rawhide webbing to give resilience. The frame was supported on four gold-sheathed lion's legs, the two at the foot being shorter than those at the head so that the bed sloped. To prevent the queen from sliding down as she slept, a foot-board, ornamented with a pattern of faience inlays was provided. We found too a pillow or head-rest of wood, sheathed in sheets of gold and silver, which we were able to reconstruct from the sheathing, all the wood having decayed. There were also in the tomb two arm-chairs similarly constructed, one of which has been rebuilt. It is low and wide so that the queen might have sat on it comfortably with her feet tucked under her, and it was supported on four lion's legs. Under each arm was a de-

35. Inlays on the floor of the tomb: detail.

36. The Queen's carrying chair of wood and sheet gold.

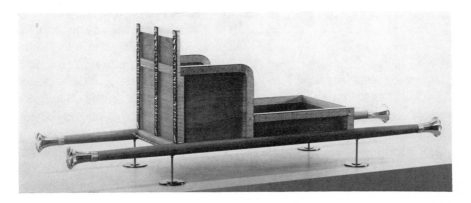

sign of grouped papyrus plants, the emblems of Lower Egypt. The other arm-chair was covered with elaborate decorations in inlay or gold, featuring under the arms a hawk with outspread wings standing on a lily, perhaps the emblem of Upper Egypt. This second chair has not as yet been rebuilt, but its design has been worked out on paper.

One of the most interesting finds in the tomb was the queen's jewel box. This lay beside the sarcophagus and had been sheathed inside and out with sheets of gold covered with a mat-pattern in relief. At first its contents were not visible, but as the clearing of the tomb progressed and some of the gold sheets from the box were removed, there came to light a series of silver bracelets (fig. 37), in-laid with butterflies in semi-precious stones, lapis lazuli, beryl, and carnelian. There had originally been twenty of these, ten for each arm, graded in size to fit from wrist to upper forearms. Later on a representation of the queen wearing these bracelets was found in the tomb, so that there can be no question as to how they were used, but at first they were thought by Dr. Reisner to have been anklets rather than bracelets.

Time and space do not permit of a detailed description here of the many other interesting and important finds from this remarkable tomb. They are fully de-scribed and discussed in the publication. *A History of the Giza Necropolis, Volume II. The Tomb of Hetep-heres*, published by the Harvard University Press in 1955 over the name of George A. Reisner, completed and revised by William Steven-son Smith. But before continuing the story a few words must be said about the identity of the remarkable gold tubes seen on the sarcophagus lid when the tomb was first opened. These tubes were actually the gold covering of a series of poles, the wood of which had disintegrated. Their lower ends were sheathed in copper and they terminated at the top in bulbous enlargements. Beside them on the lid, and fallen to the floor east of the sarcophagus were many bars and beams, together with copper-sheathed joints, tenons, hooks and staples. The study of these various large pieces after their removal from the tomb required several months, but in the end they proved to be the parts of a unique article of household furniture, none other than a demountable bed-canopy which had been placed disassembled in the chamber, apparently because it was too large to be placed there intact. The canopy consisted of a framework of heavy gold-cased beams, a series of columns, and a set of roofing poles, the whole fitted with copper-sheathed joints and held together by rawhide thongs passing through copper staples, so that the canopy could be easily taken apart, transported in

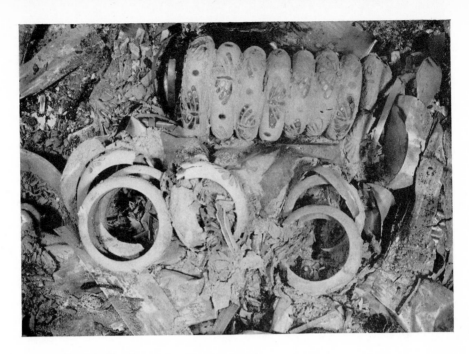

37. The Queen's silver bracelets as first uncovered.

sections, and reassembled. All around the top were a series of little hooks for the suspension of linen curtains, the latter, of course, having completely disappeared. However, the inscribed object found on the lid of the sarcophagus proved to be the decayed remains of a decorated box which had undoubtedly served as a container for the curtains when not in use (fig. 38). The two principal uprights at the front corners of the canopy bore beautiful relief inscriptions giving the names and titles of King Sneferu, and the canopy can thus be safely taken to have been a gift from her husband to Queen Hetep-heres. It was, in fact, a little portable bed-chamber which could be transported from one palace to another when the court travelled and served to afford privacy to the queen wherever she might be. When these various pieces of furniture were reconstructed with new wood on which the original gold sheathing was placed, they were set up in the Museum in Cairo and there the Queen's bed-canopy may now be seen, minus its curtains, to be sure, but equipped with her bed, arm-chair, and jewel box, much as it might have been used by this great royal lady nearly 5000 years ago. Copies of these pieces, exact in every detail, have been made and are shown in one of the Museum galleries on the ground floor in Boston (fig. 39).

Well on in the second season of our labors in the tomb, the time came for which we had all been waiting. The room at last stood empty, all but the great alabaster sarcophagus, its lid still in place. All these beautiful objects had been

38. Deposit on the sarcophagus lid. Gold and faience inlays
of a box including the cartouche of King Sneferu.

placed in the tomb for the benefit of the queen, to accompany her mummy to
the next world. Now at last the coffin was to be opened and we should see her
mortal remains, together with the jewelry and other regalia which should adorn
it. On March 3, 1927, there assembled one hundred feet underground, a distinguished company. In addition to Reisner, his two assistants and head fore-
man, there was the American Ambassador, one of the King's Chamberlains, the
Director General of Antiquities and the Chief Inspector of Antiquities for the
Giza area. At a nod from Reisner, the jacks which had been placed for the purpose began to turn. Slowly a crack appeared between the lid and the box. Little
by little it widened until one could see into the upper part of the box — nothing
was visible. As the lid slowly rose we could see further into the interior, and
finally the bottom became visible — the sarcophagus was empty! No word was
spoken, but astonishment and disappointment pervaded the chamber. Then
Reisner turned and looked at the plastered niche in the west wall of the chamber. What lay behind it? We had not long to wait for the answer. When the
plastered blocking had been removed we saw a low but deep cavity in the rock
in which stood a plain square alabaster box, its lid in place. And when it in
turn was opened it was seen to be divided into four compartments containing

all that will ever be found of the mortal remains of Hetep-heres, the four packets of her viscera which, according to Egyptian custom, had been separately embalmed and deposited in a canopic chest.

The fact that this tomb had never been entered by any thieves, that it contained the deposit originally placed in it for the benefit of the queen's spirit in the hereafter, and yet did not contain her mummy, was a puzzle of the first magnitude. How can this unique situation be explained? Let us review the facts revealed by excavation. The owner was the mother of the builder of the Great Pyramid. She had died during his reign, for she is called "Mother of the King". The deposit was made in this tomb during Cheops' reign, for mud seals bearing the insignia of his funerary officials were found in the tomb. But the arrangement of the contents was the reverse of normal. Also in clearing the mass of pottery found at the far end of the chamber, other significant facts came to light. All these vessels had originally been packed in wooden boxes in the tomb, and although these had disintegrated, it was possible to define the limits of each box by the traces of decayed wood running among the vessels. Now some of the pots were broken, and it was not too hard to discover that fragments of the same pots had been originally packed in different boxes — in other words, they had been broken before they were placed in the tomb. Another fact of great significance should also be mentioned. Chips were missing from the joint between the lid and the sarcophagus itself, and some of these chips were found by us in the boxes with the pottery, and they fitted the broken places on the sarcophagus.

All these things had to be explained, and after much thought and study, and with Reisner's profound knowledge of ancient Egyptian customs and psychology, the following account seems best to fit the circumstances and forms at least a plausible explanation of the observed facts.

Shortly after Cheops' accession to the throne his mother Hetep-heres died and, as was the custom, was buried in a tomb near the pyramid of her husband Sneferu, presumably at Dahshur some fifteen or twenty miles south of Giza. Her tomb has not been identified, but Dahshur has not as yet been thoroughly examined. Within a few years, perhaps quite soon, tomb robbers entered her tomb at night, possibly with the collusion of the watchmen, or after drugging or even murdering them. The deed was daring in the extreme, the risk was appallingly great, but the loot expected must have been extraordinarily tempting. They worked in great haste and in constant fear of discovery. Tossing aside and breaking some of the pottery, and upsetting the furniture which barred their passage

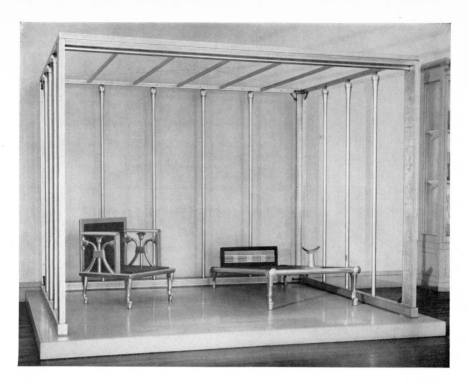

39. The Queen's bed-canopy, bed, and armchair as restored.
Wood overlaid with sheet gold.

to the sarcophagus, they roughly pried off its lid and dragged the queen's mummy
to the entrance, where moonlight afforded enough illumination for their grue-
some task. Ripping off the wrappings they despoiled the body of its jewelry,
then fled in haste into the darkness. Soon prowling jackals made off with the
dismembered remains of the queen's mummy.

   When the appalling facts were discovered by the mortuary priests the next
morning, consternation must have been indescribable. Such sacrilegious viola-
tion of the sacred tomb of the mother of the all-powerful and divine reigning
Pharoah was unthinkable. At all costs the crime must be hushed up. All trace
and knowledge of it must be suppressed. It is probable that the Vizier or Prime
Minister was secretly informed, and that he, in dread of the king's wrath, took
drastic action. He inspected the violated tomb, had the sarcophagus re-closed,
and then quite likely saw to it that everyone with knowledge of the matter was
put to death. Then one imagines that he went to the king, in any case a close
relative to whom he would have ready access in private. What did he tell him?
He may possibly have made a clean breast of the matter, relying on his relationship to protect him from retribution, for we must remember that he was
responsible for law and order in the country. But far more probably, he concealed the true facts from Pharoah. Cheops was in process of building his great

tomb, and had just begun the lesser pyramids of his wives to the east. It seems likely that the Vizier may have planted in his mind the idea of moving his mother's burial to Giza so that her spirit might be close to his own in the after-life, and perhaps share in the offerings to be made in his funerary temple which was to stand adjacent to her resting place. In any case, a shaft was dug, and a burial chamber was prepared which from its small size and unfinished state bears all the marks of haste. And when all was ready, the entire contents of the original tomb at Dahshur was transferred to the new burial place. First the pottery and stone vessels were packed in wooden boxes to conceal the damage they had suffered, and were stacked at the back of the room. Then the gold cased furniture, the jewel box and other smaller objects were placed in the western half of the chamber. The alabaster sarcophagus, unopened, was let down the shaft and placed at the east side, and on it were laid the parts of the bed-canopy and the box for its curtains. Finally, the alabaster canopic chest was placed in a niche to the west which was sealed with masonry. When all was in place workmen were set to filling in the shaft, and part way up, with due ceremonies, a food offering for the dead was solemnly placed in the niche and also sealed up.

It would be quite contrary to Egyptian beliefs about the future life of the dead for all this to have been done with the knowledge that the queen's mummy no longer existed. It would have been, from their point of view, quite useless. So we must assume that Cheops was ignorant of the fate of his mother's mummy and that the secret of the plundering of the original tomb had been kept from him. It has taken nearly five thousand years for it to be revealed.

40. The Queen's golden drinking cups.

41. Painted limestone funerary stela. H. 2 ft. 4 in.
First Intermediate Period. From Naga-ed-Der. *Expedition.*

V The Middle and New Kingdoms

THE Old Kingdom was the high point of early Egyptian culture. It was a time marked by effective governmental organization, control of the whole country by an administration centralized at the royal court, and of the concentration of power and wealth in the hands of the royal family. All talent and ability was centered at court, and art flourished under the patronage and in the service of the King, his relatives and his officials. While such conditions favored the high development of artistic talent and made possible the construction of the pyramids, economically they were hardly healthy. The wealth of the country was dissipated in non-productive labor to the glory of the king and the great nobles at court, largely in the provision of costly tombs for their spirits in the hereafter, and in the endowment of funerary priesthoods which carried on the services for the dead but performed no productive work. As the royal wealth and hence the king's power declined, he sought to purchase the loyalty and support of his officials by the granting of perquisites and lands to them and their descendants, and by the end of the Old Kingdom there had gradually grown up a powerful nobility with vested rights. By the close of the 6th Dynasty the crown had become so weakened and the landed nobility had become so powerful, that the system disintegrated and there came a time known as the First Intermediate Period, marked by anarchy in government and internecine strife among the nobles, each seeking to enlarge his own power at the expense of others. Under these conditions of ruthless struggle for survival, art as it was known in the Pyramid Age could not exist.

The Harvard–Boston Expedition excavated cemeteries of the First Intermediate Period in the region of Naga-ed-Der in Upper Egypt, opposite the ancient city of Thinis, and both the tombs and their contents are characterized by poverty and marked degeneration in the skill of artists and craftsmen. These tombs were often mere burrows excavated in a hillside, and contained a poorly made mummy in a simple wooden coffin, crudely inscribed with texts which were often badly written and well-nigh illiterate. The burials were sometimes accompanied by little wooden models of people engaged in the occupations of daily life, crudely made and lacking in any artistic quality, and sometimes too by poorly made wooden statuettes of the deceased. And whereas in the Old

Kingdom the tombs were equipped with beautiful reliefs on their chapel walls intended to provide the dead with all his needs in the next world, the burials of the First Intermediate Period contained crudely painted or carved limestone stelae which were intended to ensure to the dead the bare essentials for the future life, and to serve to identify him. Nothing could better illustrate the degradation of art during this disturbed period of ancient Egyptian history than these pathetic little monuments, of which our Expedition found a good many. They show a poorly drawn figure of the deceased, sometimes in the company of his wife or a child, facing a pile of food offerings, and accompanied by an inscription giving his name and titles and sometimes a few laudatory remarks about his virtues (fig. 41). It is interesting to note that, despite the obvious poverty of these people, their titles were often the same as those born by high officials of the Old Kingdom, such as "Chancellor of the King of Lower Eygpt", "Sole Companion", or other important indications of high rank.

This sad interlude in the greatness of ancient Egypt lasted for some two centuries, until shortly before 2000 B.C. Then the country was once more united under the crown and the authority of Pharaoh was again respected throughout Egypt. The period which we call the Middle Kingdom comprised the rulers of the 11th and 12th Dynasties (2050 to 1786 B.C.), but their power rested on a basis different from that of the Old Kingdom. The Princes of the Upper Egyptian town of Thebes (Luxor) had come to be recognized as more powerful than any of the local nobles of the other provinces or "Nomes", whom we call Nomarchs, and who had ruled their districts pretty much as they chose during the preceding period. With the advent of the 11th Dynasty, the Prince of Thebes was recognized as paramount, declared himself to be Pharaoh, and received the fealty of the other Nomarchs, forming a sort of feudal state. In return for the loyalty and service of the provincial nobility, the king gave them protection against attack from their neighbors or from external aggression, and ensured peace and order in the country. Under such improved conditions, the state of Egypt's economy revived and once more the building of temples and monumental tombs could take place and the arts could flourish again. But there was a marked difference as compared to the Old Kingdom, where every artistic talent was concentrated at court. In the Middle Kingdom, although the king could build pyramids and temples, and could command from his goldsmiths some of the most beautiful jewelry ever made in ancient Egypt, the Nomarchs were wealthy and powerful enough to have their own provincial courts which were also centers of culture.

Such a one was at Hermopolis in the 15th Nome, whose rulers were buried in rock-cut tombs in the hills on the east bank of the Nile near the modern village of El Bersheh, and here our Expedition excavated the tomb of Djehuti-Nekht, a ruler of this province in the 12th Dynasty. High up on the shoulder of the desert plateau overlooking the Nile valley (see fig. 18), the rulers of the Hare Nome had excavated their tombs and offering chapels shortly after 2000 B.C. Subsequently, earthquakes and depredations of quarrymen and tomb robbers had wrought havoc with the site, but there could still be seen traces of very fine wall decorations in the remains of the chapels. In one of these we excavated a burial shaft and found in the chamber at its base some of the great treasures which now adorn the galleries in Boston. This chamber had been rifled by ancient thieves, and the mummies of its occupants had been destroyed, but a group of magnificent great wooden coffins remained, together with many wooden models and statuettes. The outstanding object in this tomb was the great outer coffin of Djehuti-Nekht himself, the inner surfaces of which had been beautifully decorated by the hand of a master painter. Despite some damage caused by water when the ship which brought the coffin to Boston suffered a fire at sea, this is without doubt the finest painted coffin ever found. The main side, which was faced by the mummy as it lay on its side within, bears an elaborate and beautiful scene showing the owner seated before a great pile of food offerings, while an attendant burns incense before him (fig. 42). Here are ranged in profusion, dressed fowls, various cuts of meat, vegetables, fruit, flowers, loaves and cakes, and numerous vessels of varied shapes containing drink. One of the most beautiful details is the figure of a pigeon with its wings raised as if about to take flight (fig. 43). Behind the figure of the owner is pictured the door through which his spirit might enter and leave the coffin at will, and this door is framed in elaborate decorative patterns representing the multicolored hangings of matwork which ornamented the walls of the houses of wealthy Egyptians. On the opposite wall of the coffin is a long frieze of objects which would be useful to the man in the hereafter. Here we may see his bed, an assortment of headrests, a case of razors, a lavish supply of beaded jewelry, fans, mirrors, swords, bows, arrows and spears, and finally a set of carpenters' tools (fig. 44). An intriguing item is a group of white linen bags carefully labeled with the words "Royal Provisions": we shall never know what they were supposed to contain. All these decorations are most beautifully drawn and their coloring still retains much of its original harmony and freshness.

43. Wooden coffin of Djehuti-Nekht: detail, a pigeon.

44. Wooden coffin of Djehuti-Nekht: tools and weapons from the frieze of objects on the back side of the coffin.

Thrown about in great confusion by the thieves, there were many wooden objects in the tiny tomb chamber. The majority of these were models of boats of various kinds: rowing boats, boats with sails, pleasure boats with canopies to shelter the owner from the sun, a houseboat with cabin, a kitchen boat so that the lord could be supplied with meals as he journeyed on the river, and finally a war galley, equipped with spears and shields so that the soldiers who rowed it could take up arms at need for the protection of their master. One of the most beautiful things in this tomb was a model depicting a procession of three women, led by a funerary priest with libation vase and a fan (fig. 45). The women are bearing offerings to the tomb. Two of them balance on their heads baskets of food and drink and carry birds in their right hands. The third woman has unfortunately lost whatever she was carrying. The modelling of the figures is superb, and they still retain some of their original color. Finally should be noted two beautiful little statuettes from the same tomb (fig. 46). One is a finely modelled figure of a nude woman who has unfortunately lost one arm. The other also represents a woman, but she is armless and never had any legs below the knee. Her head is covered with little holes where the hair ought to be and we suppose that "real hair" had once been inserted in these holes. Her purpose is unclear — she may have been some sort of a doll with movable arms (now lost), but it seems more probable that both figures were thought of as concubines for the comfort and pleasure of their master in the afterlife.

Altogether the contents of this remarkable tomb show us that the finest work of the Middle Kingdom was by no means confined to the royal court, but that the best work of the 12th Dynasty was equally to be found in provincial centers up and down the country.

While the treasures from El Bersheh constitute the major finds made by our Expedition in Egypt of Middle Kingdom date (other fine things were found by us in the Sudan which I shall mention later), the Museum has a number of important works of art of the period which have come to it in other ways over the years. Among these I would mention here an impressive sandstone Osirid figure from Erment in Upper Egypt, a good example of this rare type of sculpture which by its style may be dated in all probability to the Middle Kingdom although it was usurped by Merenptah of the 19th Dynasty, whose name has been inserted down the front of the figure. Another fine example of Middle Kingdom sculpture, the gift of the late Denman Ross, is a quartzite head of an unknown man, bearing a considerable resemblance to the facial type which we associate with some of the kings of the 12th Dynasty. A head, or rather a fragment, with which it may be compared, is the slate portrait of King Amenemhat III which was found by us lying on the surface of the desert at Kerma in the Sudan, where we excavated a great site of Middle Kingdom date with which I shall deal more fully in the next chapter. From this same site of Kerma also comes a spirited wooden statuette representing an unidentified king of the late Middle Kingdom (fig. 48) or possibly of the Second Intermediate Period. Relatively recently, in 1950, we acquired by exchange with the Metropolitan Museum in New York, a number of beautiful fragments from the pyramid site at Lisht, which we are especially happy to have as representative of the fine relief work from the royal tombs of 12th Dynasty kings.

The Middle Kingdom lasted for some two and a half centuries, and was followed by a second period of disorganization which we call the Second Intermediate. Of this period time has left almost no trace, and it is represented in museums chiefly by a few scarabs. Once more government lost its power and there seem to have been many rival claimants to the throne. It is a time about which we have little knowledge, and the most significant fact which emerges from its shadows is that there were foreign invaders from the north-east, known as the Hyksos, who were expelled after bitter fighting by the Princes of Thebes who, at the end of the 17th Dynasty, ushered in the New Kingdom.

The New Kingdom or Empire, as it is sometimes called, found Egypt bursting out of the narrow confines of the Nile Valley to become a world power. In previous ages, while Egypt had fought her neighbors from time to time, these military adventures had been largely protective, to drive out incursions by predatory nomads along her borders, or to safeguard her trade routes into the Sudan and along the Syrian coast. But the bitter struggle against the warlike Hyksos invaders which ushered in the New Kingdom, and the pursuit of the vanquished foes into Palestine, taught the Egyptians military proficiency and the advantages to be gained by foreign conquest. The booty of successful war and the tribute exacted from vanquished rulers abroad, not to mention the acquisition of prisoners of war and the stimulus to foreign trade, brought undreamed of wealth and power to Pharaoh and to Egypt's state god, Amon-Ra, by whose favor wars were won. Thebes became the center of a world empire and the wealth of the Sudan, Palestine, Syria and on into Asia Minor and the banks of the Euphrates, filled her coffers. Under Tuthmosis III, the Napoleon of ancient Egypt, her borders reached their greatest extent, and the court of Amenhotep III was probably the most

45

46 a   46 b

45. Painted wooden procession of
offering bearers led by a priest.
L. 2 ft. 2¼ in. 12th Dynasty.
From El Bersheh. *Expedition.*

46 a. Wooden female standing.
H. 10½ in. 12th Dynasty.
from El Bersheh. *Expedition.*

46 b. Wooden female figure
without arms or lower legs.
H. 7⅜ in. 12th Dynasty.
From El Bersheh. *Expedition.*

47. Boxwood figure of a dwarf bearing a vase.
H. 2⅜ in. 18th Dynasty.
Helen and Alice Colburn Fund.

48. Wooden statuette of an
unidentified King. H. 2 ft. 1¾ in.
13th Dynasty? From Kerma. *Expedition.*

47

luxurious and ostentatious of any in the world up to that time.

Thebes was the center of this New Kingdom world, the site of great temples and palaces, and of the magnificent mortuary buildings and rock-cut tombs of the pharaohs of the time. Here our own Expedition has never excavated and so has found little representative of the period in Egypt itself. But in Egypt's foreign dominions in the Sudan we have unearthed important works of the New Kingdom, and these I shall deal with briefly in a subsequent chapter. Here I want simply to call attention to a number of objects acquired by the Museum in other ways which give us a not undistinguished representation of the period.

Among the earliest acquisitions of the Museum is a fragment from an obelisk of Queen Hatshepsut, bought at Luxor by John Lowell and presented to the Museum in 1875 by his family (see fig. 3). It gives us a fine relief portrait of this great queen of the 18th Dynasty who ruled Egypt in her own right and to whom we owe one of the most beautiful buildings at Thebes, the famed Temple of Deir el Bahari. In contrast to this fragment from a great granite monolith is the tiny boxwood figure of a dwarf bearing a vase on his shoulder, which was purchased in 1948 (fig. 47). Said to have been found at Tel el Amarna, this little toilet vessel is inscribed with the names of Akhenaten and his queen Nefertiti, whose

49. Alabaster fragment: Queen Nefertiti praying
H. of worked surface 6½ in.
18th Dynasty. From Tell el Amarna.
*Gift of Egypt Exploration Society
through the Hon. Robert Bass.*

49   50

51

50. Limestone trial piece with
profile of King Akhenaton.
H. 4¾ in. 18th Dynasty. From Tell el Amarna.
*Gift of Egypt Exploration Society
through Mrs. Charles Gaston Smith and Group.*

51. Sandstone head of a king,
perhaps Tut-ankh-Amen.
H. 11⅝ in. 18th Dynasty.
Gift of Miss Mary S. Ames.

52. Limestone relief representing a Nile god. H. 1 ft. 6 in.
18th Dynasty. Probably from Thebes. *Gift of Edward W. Forbes.*

53. Red jasper face from an inlay probably representing King Seti I. H. 1⅛ in. 19th Dynasty? *Harriet Otis Cruft Fund.*

55. Group of faience and one bronze vase of the New Kingdom. H. of polychrome vase with slender neck 9¼ in. 18th Dynasty, faiences from Abydos, *Gift of Egypt Exploration Fund*, the bronze from Semna, *Expedition.*

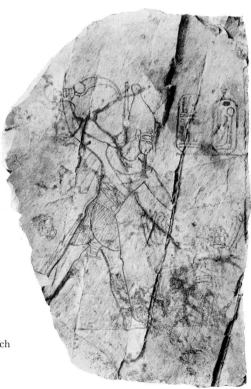

54. Limestone ostrakon with ink sketch of a king slaying captives. H. 12 in. 20th Dynasty. *Gift of Denman W. Ross.*

55

monotheistic revolution rocked Egypt to its foundations and left a legacy of
strangely beautiful works of art, the best known of which is the famous bust of
his queen formerly in Berlin. We too have a portrait of this beautiful woman, a
small fragment of a relief in alabaster which shows the queen praying to Akhenaton's god Aten (fig. 49). Of the king himself, we have a limestone fragment from
a sculptor's trial sketch (fig. 50), but the hand which carved it was that of a
master. Both pieces were acquired from the Egypt Exploration Society — which
excavated Akhenaton's capital city of Amarna. The most famous of Akhenaton's
immediate successors was the boy king Tut-Ankh-Amen, whom we would barely
have known were it not for the sensational find in 1923 of his unplundered tomb
by Carter and Lord Carnarvon. Those treasures are housed in the Cairo Museum,
but we have a fine limestone head of a young king once lent to us by our former
Honorary Curator, Joseph Lindon Smith, and given to us by Miss Mary S. Ames
in 1911. Comparing this head with the known portraits of Tut-Ankh-Amen leaves
little doubt that he is the king represented (fig. 51). Those who have seen the
Tut-Ankh-Amen finds in Cairo will remember a striking group representing the
king standing on the back of a black panther. This find has enabled us to understand a beautiful wooden figure of a striding black panther (see fig. 10) given
to us many years ago by Theodore M. Davis, for on its back there remain two
wooden dowels, which once served to attach a statuette, in this case that of King
Tuthmosis IV, for the figure was found in his tomb.

The last king of the 18th Dynasty is not very well known. His name was Ay, and there exists a colossal statue of him seated on a throne, the latter badly damaged. One of the fragments from this battered monument was given to the Museum recently by Edward W. Forbes. It is a beautiful relief of a so-called Nile god (fig. 52) and once formed part of the decoration of the throne just mentioned, on which two figures of the Nile were shown binding the papyrus of Lower Egypt and the lily of Upper Egypt around the hieroglyph which signifies unity.

Two further rulers of the New Kingdom are represented in our galleries. The first of these objects chronologically speaking, was bought as recently as 1940. It is a tiny relief face of King Seti I in jasper (fig. 53), which once formed part of an inlaid figure of the king, and is a fine example of the lapidary's art. His successor on the throne was Ramesses the Great, second to bear the name, and we have had for many years a large seated statue of him, found in the 1880s by the Egypt Exploration Society in the Delta (see fig. 6). While in no sense a great work of art, it is a representative example of the enormous number of statues produced by this king, who was one of the great masters of self-advertising of the ancient world. Ramesses II is represented again by a fragmentary stela, acquired in 1909, on which he is shown seated receiving the homage of his vizier, Pa-Ser. Another vizier of this king, Pa-Ra-Hotep by name, is shown seated on the ground with arms crossed over his knees in a granite statue which came to us in 1903.

I spoke in Chapter I of a little head excavated by Petrie, which we acquired many years ago and which was thought by the excavator to be of Ptolemaic date (see fig. 35). But recently a member of our Department was able to prove that it fitted onto a torso in the Louvre inscribed with the name of Amenhotep II of the 18th Dynasty. We have another similar case, though not this time royal. A grey granite head of a scribe, given to us in 1942 by Mrs. Richard M. Saltonstall, has formed the subject of a careful study by our former Assistant Curator, Bernard V. Bothmer, who has shown that it most probably belonged to a headless figure in the same material now in the British Museum, a statue of one Amenhotep, son of Hapu, who lived in the reign of Amenhotep III.

Space will not permit mention here of many other interesting and important objects in our collections which illustrate the art and culture of the New Kingdom. We shall have to limit ourselves to three further examples. The first of these is what is called in the profession an ostracon, a term properly applied in

Classical archaeology to a potsherd, but in Egypt used to describe a class of limestone flake employed by Egyptian artists for making preliminary sketches or for trying out designs. Such a one shows on one side a spirited sketch in black pigment of a familiar subject — the king with uplifted sword about to dispatch a group of suppliant captives whom he grasps firmly by the hair (fig. 54). The cartouches roughly sketched into the scene are those of one of the Ramesside kings of the 20th Dynasty. On the reverse side is a fragmentary scene of conquered foreign lands bound to the royal war chariot, symbolized by two figures, one a negro representing the South, and the other a Syrian representing the North.

Egyptian craftsmanship was versatile and it is in the so-called minor arts that we are able to appreciate the skill and taste of their artistry sometimes better than in larger and more formal objects. I have spoken already of the little toilet-vase of Amenhotep III and Queen Tiy which, despite its tiny size, is full of vigor and charm (see fig. 48). Another example of the skill of Egyptian woodcarvers is a fragmentary toilet box bought in 1949, which may be dated to the early 18th Dynasty. In the *Bulletin* for December, 1952, Dr. William Stevenson Smith discusses this rare and beautiful little object, the carving of which bears evidence of the influence of Aegean art on Egyptian craftsmanship during the New Kingdom.

While Egyptian pottery is seldom decorated and cannot be compared in quality with the magnificent painted vases of Classical Greece, the vessels of glazed faience made in the Nile valley are often works of great artistic merit and highly skilled workmanship. Our Expedition found many fragmentary examples of such vessels at Kerma in the Sudan, which may be assigned to the Middle Kingdom, a site about which I shall have something to say in the next chapter. One fine example of such vases, out of a private tomb of the 18th Dynasty at Abydos, came to us from the Egypt Exploration Society in 1909. Although incomplete, it is a striking illustration of the elaborate polychrome faience vessels which were in fashion at the time (fig. 55). Its tall neck and papyriform mouth, and the bands of multicolored conventionalized designs around the shoulder are thoroughly Egyptian in character.

56. Kerma. Ruins of the 12th Dynasty mud-brick fort.

VI The Sudan I

Kerma and the Cataract Forts

THE preceding three chapters have been devoted to the work of our Expedition in Egypt itself, but from 1914 to 1932, a great part of its work took place further south — beyond the borders of Egypt proper — in what is called the Sudan, or rather that part of the Sudan which lies between the Second Cataract of the Nile and Khartoum at the junction of the Blue and White Niles. So I shall devote this and the next two chapters to our work in that area — work which has brought to the Museum a great many beautiful objects, but even more important, has opened up a whole new chapter of ancient history.

From the border of Egypt at the Second Cataract the Nile flows southward (see fig. 13) through a region which is barren, rocky and almost uninhabitable. It is known today to the local people as the "Belly of Rocks" and the river is broken by stretches of swift water and numerous islands. Beyond the Second Cataract there is a stretch of navigable river, and then comes the Third Cataract. Beyond that the Nile again becomes free for navigation where it takes a great bend to the east and then to the north-east as far as the Fourth Cataract, at which point it is quite impassable, turns east once more, and then south again, so that a great S is formed from above the Third to above the Fourth Cataract. Thereafter the river again takes its normal course southward to Khartoum, passing through the Fifth and Sixth Cataracts on the way.

Throughout this area our Expedition has carried out excavations at a number of places. Five forts in the Second Cataract area were examined, only two of which I can deal with here. They were occupied at intervals from the 12th Dynasty to Kushite times. Then just above the Third Cataract we excavated the site of Kerma, a trading post dating to the 12th Dynasty and continuing for some time thereafter. Going on upstream we come to a group of ancient sites just below the Fourth Cataract, of which the three examined by us are known as El Kurru, a cemetery of the early Kushite Period; Gebel Barkal, a complex of temples and pyramids dating from the 18th Dynasty through to the Meroitic Period; and Nuri, the great royal cemetery of the rulers of Kush from the 25th Dynasty to about 300 B.C. Finally, between the Fifth and Sixth Cataracts, the ancient town of Meroë lies on the east bank of the river, and in the desert east of the town there are three cemeteries which contain royal and private tombs ranging in date all the way from early Kushite to the end of the Meroitic Period, or shortly before A. D. 340.

Now I want to discuss our excavations at Kerma and at the Second Cataract forts of Semna and Kumma. Let us take Kerma first because historically it is the earliest of these sites.

East of the river at Kerma stretches a wide flat plain, from which there rise the remains of two large mud-brick structures. Near them, and scattered widely over the plain are many low circular mounds, some large and many small. They rise only slightly above the present surface and are covered with small stones which were placed there to protect them from wind erosion. This is the great cemetery started in the Egyptian 12th Dynasty and continuing to be used probably for several centuries thereafter, and it contains the tombs of those who inhabited an important trading center where the products of the south were gathered for shipment to Egypt. One of the great brick structures mentioned before appears to have been the fortified headquarters of the place (fig. 56), no doubt with an Egyptian garrison for the protection of the Egyptians in charge of the outpost. The excavation of the tombs at Kerma yielded a rich and largely un-Egyptian group of finds, some of which I will speak of presently. I want to describe the tombs themselves, for they were of a type quite new to Egyptian archaeology. These circular mounds or tumuli, do not appear to have been generally provided with offering-places as was the case in Egypt. In them the dead were placed un-mummified upon a wooden bed, lying in a natural sleeping position. They were accompanied in the grave by weapons, personal ornaments, pottery vessels and food, but they had not the traditional amulets, models, and many of the other things normal to Egyptian graves of the period. But most striking of all, the richer people were accompanied in the grave by one or more attendants, wives or servants (fig. 59); people killed and buried with their master so as to serve him in the next world. These people were not Egyptians but local Sudanese, and here for the first time we got a clear picture of the differences between their burial customs and those of the Egyptians. I want to emphasize these differences because they will be very significant as we go along. Essentially they were these: first, the use of a tumulus or mound to mark the burial place, instead of a mastaba, pyramid or rock-cut tomb; second, no mummification and none of the appurtenances of such Egyptian burials — no canopic jars to contain the viscera, no shawabti figures, none of the usual Egyptian amulets; third, burial in a natural sleeping posture on a bed, not in a coffin as in Egypt; and fourth, the use of human sacrifice, a practice quite foreign to dynastic Egypt. The largest of the Kerma tumuli were impressive monuments (fig. 57). Their shape was maintained not only by the deposit of stones on the surface, but by a network of mud-brick retaining walls covered by the tumulus. Down the center ran a corridor (fig. 58), and in the biggest mound of all we found over a hundred people sacrificed at the funeral, some apparently buried alive if we may judge by the distorted position of some of their bodies.

And now what of the objects from Kerma of which we have so many in the Museum. First of all there were the beds on which the dead were laid, made of wood and usually far gone in decay. From the many warped and damaged examples found we have been able to make a replica to show what they were like when new. The four legs were carved to represent bull's legs and those at the head end were longer than those at the foot so that the bed sloped slightly, though not as much as the bed from the tomb of Queen Hetep-heres which we saw earlier (see fig. 39). Like this latter bed, there was a footboard, and this was ornamented with bone or ivory inlays, of which we found a great many in a wide variety. The frame of the bed was laced with rawhide thongs on which the body lay, and these pieces of furniture showed a considerable refinement of design which could not be appreciated from the warped and distorted originals (fig. 60). I shall come to the inlays themselves presently, but first I want to describe the pottery of which great quantities were found in these graves.

Previous to our excavations at Kerma, sporadic examples of a peculiarly fine type of vessel had been found which archaeologists had not been able to identify. At Kerma we found this type by the hundreds, they are bell-shaped cups or beakers, black on the inside and partway down the outside from the rim, and red below, highly burnished, and extremely thin and hard, so finely made that the best of them have a bell-like ring when tapped (fig. 61 a,b). In many of the graves these vessels were nested in stacks and had been enclosed in string nets, some of which showed elaborate patterns. In some cases too there were tall, horizontally-ribbed vessels simulating in one piece a stack of these beakers (fig. 61d). Other peculiar types which are certainly of local origin suggest animal forms — one with a spout in the form of a bull's head, one with a ram's head, another perhaps representing either a hippopotamus or a pig, and one rather globular pot on feet, with an up-curving neck, which was clearly supposed to suggest an ostrich chick, for it has modelled on it little rudimentary wings and a tail. There were also an interesting group of polychrome painted vessels, some

57. One of the large circular tumuli at Kerma before excavation.

of which were clearly derived from basket-work prototypes both in form and decoration (fig. 62b), while others had painted scenes on them, including one with a design of a man attacked by two lions (fig. 62a). These painted vessels have, unfortunately, suffered considerably from fading since they were unearthed, but their designs were copied in water-color drawings soon after they were found, and these drawings are shown in the Museum together with the pots themselves.

In addition to the products of the local potters, there was clearly another important industry at Kerma, that of the makers of faience and blue glazed quartz. A great quantity of glazed faience vessels were found, unfortunately almost all represented by fragments, together with many objects of glazed quartz, and not a few indications that the glazing was done on the spot, as evidenced by many bits of stone partly covered with glaze which had been used to support objects in the furnaces. Perhaps the most attractive of these faience fragments is a portion of a glazed pot in dark blue with a scene of fluttering birds in lighter blue (see fig. 61c).

Many of the Kerma burials were clearly those of men, if we may judge by the frequency with which they were provided with swords or daggers. These weapons too were of an unfamiliar type with long thin bronze blades, rather

58. The same tumulus after excavation: mud-brick retaining walls
and long corridor which contained sacrificial burials.

59. One of the smaller burials at Kerma:
the body on a bed
with human sacrifices below.

60. Copy of a wooden funerary bed from Kerma. L. 6 ft.
Rawhide lacing, wooden footboard with bone inlays. *Director's Contingent Fund.*

inadequate wooden grips and elongated bone or ivory projections above the grip. They seem clearly to have been ceremonial or dress weapons rather than ones intended for use in warfare. The graves also frequently contained bronze razors, originally with wooden handles, and sometimes carefully placed in wooden sheaths to protect the blade. Another interesting class of object was what appear to be military decorations, found normally in pairs. There are passages in Egyptian literature in which people boasting of their accomplishments and recording royal favor, use the expression "His majesty gave me two flies". We found these flies in graves at Kerma, sometimes made of ivory and sometimes of bronze, clearly two classes of this reward for service. I can do no more than mention a number of other interesting things from Kerma, such as basketry, leather work and objects of giraffe hair; nor can I illustrate many of the ostrich feather fans of which a good many were found, because so few of them survived transport to Boston when the boxes in which they were packed were soaked in sea-water owing to a fire on the ship. I do want, however, to mention the bone and ivory inlays from the footboards of the many beds, because they are of special interest (fig. 63). These inlays, which were let into wooden panels, are mostly figures of animals, and were clearly of local manufacture, for although such typically Egyptian figures as the vulture with outspread wings and the demi-god Thoeris occur fairly often, the great majority are creatures not normally seen in Egypt itself. Most clearly coming from Sudanese contexts are the elephant, the giraffe, sometimes represented with wings, the crocodile, the ostrich, and the ostrich-chick. A group of two goats browsing on a tree is reminiscent of similar motifs from Mesopotamia, and other animals, while they were

61 a   c   d

61. Pottery and faience vessels from Kerma. Middle Kingdom. *Expedition.* (Bell beaker H. 4⅛ in.: Spouted jar H. 4⅝ in.: Ribbed beaker H. 8⅝ in.: Faience bowl fragment H. 4 in.).

b

62. Two painted pottery vessels from Kerma. Middle Kingdom. (Basket form H. without lid 3½ in.: Jar H. 5⅝ in.). *Expedition.*

62 a   b

63. Bone inlays from various footboards of funerary beds at Kerma. Middle Kingdom. *Expedition.*

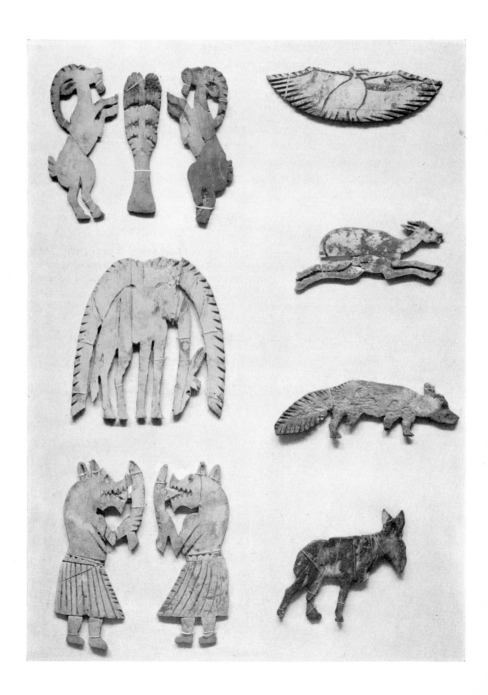

certainly known at Kerma, are not exclusive to these southern lands — the don-
key, fox, hyena, turtle, and various types of antelope, including one charming
one of a running gazelle.

Despite these indications of the local source of many of the objects from Kerma,
the site also yielded things clearly imported, for they are quite typical of 12th
Dynasty Egyptian style. The most important of these, and one of our outstanding
treasures, is the large black granite seated statue of the Lady Sennuwy (fig. 64),
wife of a man named Hepjefa, who was nomarch of Assiut in the 12th Dynasty.
This beautiful figure, together with fragments of a statue of her husband, was
found in one of the largest of the tumuli at Kerma, and led Reisner to the con-
clusion that her husband, despite the fact that he had prepared for himself a
fine tomb at Assiut, had been governor at Kerma, had died there, and had been
buried in the Sudanese manner on the spot together with many human sacrifices. It is certainly very surprising that an Egyptian nobleman who died in a
foreign land would fail to have his body sent home for decent burial according
to Egyptian custom; we know from Egyptian literature that burial in alien soil
and according to the customs of the barbarians was extremely distasteful, and
some scholars have questioned Reisner's conclusions accordingly. Nevertheless,
it is hard to account for the presence of two large statues of this Egyptian and
his wife deep in a foreign land, unless they had been brought there by his order
for use in his tomb. This figure of the Lady Sennuwy was the largest and finest
piece of sculpture at Kerma, but a number of statuettes and fragments of smaller
figures of Egyptians, including kings of the 12th Dynasty were also found, indicating the presence there of Egyptians. Small statues of the reigning king are
always to be expected in any center of Egyptian influence abroad, much as portraits of the sovereign are to be seen in British embassies and consulates today;
they were the symbols of Egyptian power abroad.

The trade with Kerma necessitated communication down through the wild
and barren reaches of the Second Cataract to Egypt, and this had to be protected against interference by the wild nomads who lived largely by raiding.
And so it was only natural that this line of communication should have been
guarded by a chain of forts, garrisoned by Egyptian soldiers. Of the five such
fortified places excavated by our Expedition, the two southernmost stood at the
head of the Second Cataract, where the river, passing through a narrow gorge
between rocky bluffs, breaks into rapids which necessitate the man-handling of
boats passing through in either direction. Here stood the two forts of Kumma,

on the east bank, and Semna opposite it on the west side of the river. (fig. 65). Originally built in the 12th Dynasty, they were re-built after the second Intermediate Period in the 18th Dynasty, and were in more or less constant use from then until at least the 25th Dynasty. The situation was well suited to its purpose. Because of the waterless and rugged country in this region all travel must pass either by water, where it was checked by the rapids, or along the banks of the river by land. The two forts, standing high above the river, could control passage by either route. They were surrounded by massive mud-brick walls which even today, despite many centuries of wind erosion, stand as prominent landmarks. On the river side the steep rocky slope prevented assault, while at Semna on the western, northern, and southern sides, a dry moat and a glacis gave further check to possible assailants who would have found themselves subjected to murderous fire from the main walls while trying to negotiate these obstacles. Within the walls the space was tightly packed with buildings of mudbrick: barracks for the soldiers and their families, administrative offices, and store-rooms for supplies. The focal point in each of the forts was a small temple, that of the 18th Dynasty, built of stone and richly embellished with reliefs. Traces of a 12th Dynasty sanctuary were found in each of the forts, but these had been so overlaid with later buildings that little remained. At Semna itself, however, an impressive building of the 25th Dynasty still stood — the temple built there by King Taharqa, the great Kushite ruler who controlled both the Sudan and Egypt itself. On the western bank the land was somewhat less rugged than on the eastern, and here ran the road for land travel, passing right through the fort by means of gates at its north and south ends. At both forts, presumably kept provisioned with food against attack, water was obtained by means of a stairway descending steeply to the river, and protected on either side against enemy fire by high walls, and at Semna passing also in part through a tunnel built of stone right over its upper portion. We cannot say how long the tour of duty at these Egyptian outposts may have been, but we can be sure that some at least of the soldiers stationed there were accompanied by their families. Several cemeteries which served the garrison were excavated by us and they included the graves of both women and children. From the forts of Semna-Kumma it was possible for the garrison, looking out to the north, to see a third fort some two or three miles downstream, which stood on an island in the river, known as Uronarti, also excavated by our Expedition. We have dug two other forts in this area, still further north, and it seems probable that all of these outposts, of which

64. Black granite statue of the Lady Sennuwy. H. 5 ft. 6¾ in.
12th Dynasty. From Kerma. *Expedition.*

there may originally have been others, were within signalling distance of each other, and so could lend each other support at need.

While the primary interest of our excavations at these forts lay in the light it shed on military architecture and on the system of communication with Egypt, they also yielded a not inconsiderable number of Museum objects. At Kumma, built into the foundations of the existing temple, we found two blocks of white sandstone decorated with reliefs (fig. 66). These bore the name of King Tuthmosis III and formed part of the decoration in the corner of one of the rooms in an earlier temple on the site, later re-used by Amenhotep II as underpinning for the walls of his temple. The subject treated is the king making offerings to the ram-headed god Khnum. Another fine example of temple relief comes from Semna and shows King Tuthmosis II before the local god, Dedwen. One of the important bits of evidence proving that the forts already existed in the 12th Dynasty is a granite grave stela from the tomb of an Egyptian military commander, the General Amenemhat, who evidently died while serving at Semna. A number of little statuettes of private persons, no doubt made for their tombs or set up in the local temple so as to share in the offerings to the gods, were found, as also a fragmentary figure of an 18th Dynasty King, probably an official statuette of the ruler in this foreign outpost. These are among the examples of Egyptian sculpture found in the forts.

One of the most interesting class of objects found were the scarabs and the impressions made by them on mud sealings. The Egyptian scarab had several purposes, but perhaps the majority of them during the New Kingdom were used as personal or official seals. In a population the great majority of whom were unable to read and write, it was important that people should have a way of signing their names or indicating ownership. Many scarabs were used for this purpose, much as an earlier generation of Americans and Europeans used signet rings. Even today the illiterate majority of Egyptian peasants have personal seals engraved with their names, with which they sign letters and documents, including the payroll when they receive their wages. When an ancient Egyptian sent a letter or a parcel by a messenger, he would tie it up firmly with string put a pellet of mud over the knot and make an impression in the mud with his scarab. The parcel or letter could not be tampered with until the recipient broke the hardened mud pellet. Now there was naturally much sending and receiving of letters and parcels, both official and personal, at these garrisons, and we found hundreds of these mud sealings discarded from them after they were opened,

65. The two forts at Semna:
View looking NW. over Kumma Fort
with Semna Fort beyond the Nile
in the background.

66

67

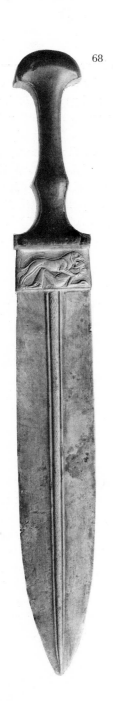

68

69 a   b

66. Sandstone reliefs of King Tuthmosis III. H. 2 ft. 10⅞ in.
18th Dynasty. Kumma Fort. *Expedition.*

67. Bronze axe-head. L. 4¾ in. 18th Dynasty. From Semna.
Expedition, now in Khartoum.

68. Bronze dagger. L. 16¼ in. 18th Dynasty. From Semna.
Expedition, now in Khartoum.

69 a & b. Two Bronze Menat-amulets. One in Boston H. 5½ in.
The other in Khartoum. New Kingdom. Semna. *Expedition.*

as well as a great many of the scarabs with which such impressions were made. In general these were of two kinds: official seals bearing the title of the government official who used them, and often his name as well, and personal seals with either the owner's name, or frequently an individual pattern which was unique and sufficed to identify its owner. No two of these scarabs are ever exactly alike, but they fall into a number of well defined classes such as scroll patterns, groups of signs mixed with abstract designs, sometimes the name of the king combined with other symbols — in fact in so great a variety that it would require a lengthy article to describe them. The point I want to make is simply that the finding of these scarabs and sealings, dull as they may be from the point of view of Museum display, has had considerable value for our better understanding of life at these forts in the New Kingdom.

From the cemeteries at Semna and Kumma come a number of striking and beautiful objects, although, as was only to be expected at such a place, there were few, if any, graves of really rich or prominent people. Being primarily inhabited by soldiers, it was only to be expected that weapons would be found. The outstanding examples are both in Khartoum and were not assigned to Boston, but they are illustrated here from our Expedition photographs because of their exceptional interest. One is a battle axe-head of bronze of openwork design (fig. 67) featuring a figure of a lion leaping upon a horned animal, perhaps a species of buck or antelope. This is perhaps hardly a very practical fighting tool, rather it may be thought of as a semi-ornamental parade weapon. Of possibly more practical utility is a bronze dagger with a wooden handle with little relief scenes on either side just below the grip: on one side a lion attacking a negro (fig. 68), and on the other a parallel scene with a Syrian foreigner instead of a negro. Thus, these two little scenes are symbolic of Egypt conquering her enemies of the south and the north, a subject very commonly treated in Egyptian art over many centuries. Of more intimate nature, and perhaps coming from the graves of women, were other things: two charming little bronze objects called Menats featuring the figure of the goddess Hathor, and a cow, her distinctive animal (fig. 69). These are things of an amuletic nature associated with the goddess of pleasure and used in her cult dances. Then there are two fine mirrors, the handle of one showing a graceful figure of a nude girl (fig. 70) and the other with a wooden handle bearing a representation of the god, Bes, patron of the toilet.

70. Bronze mirror. H. 8⅞ in. New Kingdom. From Semna. *Expedition.*

71. View of Gebel Barkal, the "Holy Mountain," looking NW.

VII The Sudan II

The Napatan Kingdom of Kush;
Barkal, Kurru, Nuri

WE MUST NOW move still further south to the country just below the Fourth
Nile Cataract, and we shall jump in time from the Middle to the New Kingdom and even later. From 1916 to 1919 the Expedition excavated three important sites in this region: the Temples at Gebel Barkal, the early Kushite
cemetery of El Kurru, and the later necropolis of Nuri, all of which were associated with the ancient city of Napata which formed the capital of Kush
during the Egyptian New Kingdom and throughout the early phases of the
Kingdom of Kush.

During the Second Intermediate Period, that time of chaos which intervened
between the Middle and New Kingdoms, we are without any knowledge of conditions in the Sudan. But in the 18th and 19th Dynasties we have considerable
information from Egyptian sources. During this period of Egyptian imperial ex-
pansion and military power, contact with the south became more and more intimate and we find Egypt taking actual possession of the Sudan and ruling the
country through Viceroys who represented the King of Egypt and who bore the
title "King's Son of Kush". I suppose the situation was in some respects parallel
to Imperial British rule in India during the last century, and that the administrative organization and most of the higher officials were Egyptian. Certainly
Egyptian culture was thoroughly established, especially in the matter of religion. Amun, the official state god of Egypt, had a great temple at Gebel Barkal,
the "Holy Mountain", second only to the parent shrine of the god at Thebes.
The site of this temple, which we excavated, is striking. It lies close against the
eastern cliff of a great butte-like mountain, the most prominent landmark in the
area, which had certainly been a holy place from ancient times (fig. 71). We do
not know when a temple was first built on this site, but by the 18th Dynasty a
great granite stela was erected here to commemorate the conquests of Tuthmosis III in Palestine and Syria, a monument of great historical importance
which is in the Museum. The ruins of the great temple, which still exist (fig. 72),
give evidence of building by Ramesses II of the 19th Dynasty, of extensions
under the early kings of the 25th Dynasty, and of additions, repairs, and recon-

structions well down to the Meroitic period; for a stela in our Seventh Egyptian Gallery, which may be dated to the second half of the Second Century B.C., was found in this temple. A great black granite altar erected by King Taharqa of the 25th Dynasty still stands in the sanctuary today, but a somewhat smaller altar set up by a later king of Kush in an adjacent building has been brought to Boston (fig. 73). It weighs seven tons and may be seen in our Mastaba Gallery, where it had to be placed on a special steel-reinforced base lest it sink through the floor.

During its long history the great temple saw invasions and at least partial destruction and rebuilding. In 591 B.C., Psameticus II invaded the area and despoiled the temple. He broke up the statues of Kushite Kings which had stood in its great court and we found them thrown out to north and south. Three of these, reconstructed from their scattered fragments, now stand in the Museum, rare examples of monumental Kushite sculpture (fig. 74). They had originally been ornamented with bracelets, anklets and necklaces of gold leaf laid over the stone, for although these have now disappeared, their positions are marked by the roughening of the granite to receive the gold overlays.

A few miles down stream from Barkal lies the early Kushite cemetery of El Kurru, a sadly ruined site (fig. 75), but one of great interest, for here our Expedition found the tombs of all but one of the Kings of the Egyptian 25th Dynasty, those rulers of Kush who turned the tables on declining Egypt and conquered their erstwhile overlord. The place is not impressive to look at, for the superstructures of the tombs have almost disappeared to furnish building materials for the adjacent village, yet this site proved to be one of the most important ever excavated by our Expedition: it threw a flood of light on a hitherto little known period of ancient history, and yielded some of the most beautiful of the small objects which we have in the Museum.

In the last chapter I spoke of the peculiar Sudanese burial customs which we found at Kerma, dating to about 2000 B.C. or a little later. These were essentially un-Egyptian and were marked by the use of a circular burial mound or tumulus, the interment of the dead in a natural sleeping position lying on a bed and without mummification, and the prevalence of the barbaric practice of human sacrifice. Now the earliest burials at Kurru may be dated to about 850 B.C., some thousand years later than the Kerma tombs, yet despite the lapse of time, during much of which the country had been under strong Egyptian influence and subjected to Egyptian rule, these graves show many of the same peculiari-

72. The Great Temple of Amon at Barkal, after excavation,
looking down from top of Gebel Barkal.

ties as those at Kerma. Here too we found circular tumuli and evidence that
the dead were placed on beds without any signs of mummification. There was,
however, no trace of human sacrifice, and it seems evident that this barbaric
Sudanese practice had by this time been abandoned under the influence of the
more advanced civilization of Egypt. The excavations at Kurru revealed a most
interesting evolution in the form of the tomb structure, a relatively rapid one,
for the last major tomb in the primary series was built about 650 B.C., only two
centuries after the cemetery was founded. Following the first circular gravel
tumulus, we found in succession circular mounds cased in stone with a tiny
chapel on the surface facing east, a circular mound encased in a rectangular
masonry structure which we call a mastaba, and then the circular mound dis-
appears and the rectangular mastaba becomes the rule. In all these tombs burial
was made in a simple pit beneath the center of the superstructure, which was
constructed over the grave after the burial. These earlier tombs on the site covered
about six generations, the last and largest of them probably being the tomb of
Kashta (fig. 76), the Kushite prince who is known to have invaded Egypt itself just prior to 750 B.C.

73

The excavation of these earlier tombs at Kurru, which had been very heavily plundered, did not supply us with any inscribed material which would reveal the names of their owners, but they did yield a number of solid gold beads and amulets overlooked by the ancient thieves (fig. 77). This recalls the fact that the land of Kush was gold mining country, called by the Egyptians "The Gold Lands of Amon", no doubt one of the reasons why the country was of such interest to Egypt during the New Kingdom.

When we come to the later burials at Kurru we find a marked change in their character. The mastaba form of superstructure, a square building with steeply sloping sides and a flat top, was replaced by the true pyramid, rising to a point reminiscent of the royal tombs of the Egyptian Old and Middle Kingdoms. The burial place beneath this building was reached by a stairway descending into the rock, and the sepulchral chamber was either roofed with a stone corbel vault or was excavated in the rock in such a way that the whole building and burial place could be prepared during the owner's lifetime (fig. 78). With the advent of this more complex form of tomb there went a modification of the local burial customs more in keeping with the practice of contemporary Egypt. The Egyptian practice of mummification appears, as is evidenced from the finding of canopic jars, those vessels of specialized form in which certain organs of the dead were separately embalmed. Yet despite the introduction of the mummy,

73. Granite altar of King Atlanersa.
H. 3 ft. 9¼ in. ca. 645 B.C.
From Barkal (Temple 700). *Expedition.*

74. Granite statue of King Aspelta.
H. 10 ft. 1⅝ in. ca. 570 B.C.
From Temple of Amon, Barkal. *Expedition.*

74

75. The Cemetery of El Kurru, looking west.

76. The tomb of King Kashta at El Kurru, looking west.

which in contemporary Egypt was buried in a coffin, the old Kushite practice of burial on a bed was retained. This bed was now placed on a stone bench, the four corners of which were cut out to permit the legs of the bed to rest on the floor. In one tomb we found two of the bed legs, made of bronze, still in position although the rest of the bed, being made of wood, had long since decayed (fig. 79). One of these is now in Boston; it incorporates the figure of a goose in the round, with the leg of the bed rising above its back, a beautiful example of bronze casting. One further class of object appeared now for the first time at Kurru. These are little blue faience figures of a mummy, known to Egyptologists as shawabti figures. They are characteristic of Egyptian burials from the New Kingdom to Roman times, and were placed in the tombs to act as substitutes for the dead in the next world should the gods call upon him to perform various kinds of manual labor. Now these shawabti figures are inscribed with incantations which explain their purpose, and the name of the owner forms part of the inscription. Through the finding of these figures the excavators were able to identify the owners of these later tombs at Kurru, which proved to be those of most of the kings and queens of the 25th Dynasty of Egypt, that family of Sudanese chieftains who conquered and ruled over Egypt for several generations. The first of these was named Piankhy, who gained control of Egypt about 730 B.C., and both he and his successors had long been known from inscriptions on monuments in Egypt. Here then we found the tombs of this line of Pharaohs, the descendants of the early Kushite princes of Kurru, who returned to their home-land for burial. And this newly learned fact largely explains the changes from earlier custom found in their tombs, for the earliest of the pyramids at Kurru, the first evidence of mummification, and the first use of shawabti figures, corresponds exactly with that of the first prince of Kush to become Pharaoh of Egypt. The intimate contact with the sophisticated culture of Egypt, acquired by conquest, led to the Egyptianizing of their burial practices and funerary beliefs. Only the old native custom of burial on a bed survived for a time as a link with their more primitive past.

So much for the historical importance of Kurru. I cannot pass on to the next part of my story, however, without a word about some of the very interesting things found in these tombs which are now in our Museum in Boston. I have already mentioned the unusually rich finds of gold beads and amulets from the early tombs on the site (see fig. 77). From the burial of a queen of one of the kings of the 25th Dynasty came a beautiful solid gold collar forming a complete circle, which could be opened by two hinges through which gold pins were thrust (fig. 80). The ornament is simple but effective and is decorated in front with a kneeling winged human figure in relief, balanced behind by a scarab. A somewhat more utilitarian find comes from the tomb of Shabako, second king of the Dynasty. It is a bronze disc mirror with a gilded silver handle on which are depicted in high relief four standing figures of Egyptian goddesses (fig. 81). The tombs of the queens buried at Kurru yielded an unusually rich and varied group of amulets, some of which were of conventional types familiar to us from contemporary Egypt, while others had a distinctively African character (fig. 82). Among the latter were a number of winged female figures with enormously fat legs, showing a love of steatopygy which we shall see again in the royal reliefs of a later period. A unique amulet is the little rock crystal ball surmounted by a golden head of the goddess Hathor (fig. 83), provided with a suspension ring so that it could be worn around the neck. To be classed also as an amulet is the marble figure of a cat in the round, an exceptionally beautiful example of small scale sculpture in the best Egyptian style (fig. 84). Although one ear is missing, both were originally pierced to receive little gold ear-rings (now lost). Finally I must mention another unique find at Kurru, which we are in the habit of calling the "cocktail table". It comes from the tomb of King Piankhy, where it was found crushed and broken by falls of rock from the roof. Skillful work by the Museum's Research Laboratory has restored it to its original appearance and it now stands in one of the Study Rooms on the ground floor (fig. 85). It was undoubtedly a libation stand, and consists of a circular bronze tray with four bronze cups attached to its rim, the whole resting on a tall conical base and having a central rod rising above the tray which terminates in a palm leaf capital bearing a shallow cup.

So much for Kurru. We must now move on to the great cemetery of Nuri, which lies across the river and a few miles above Gebel Barkal. This is a large group of pyramids isolated behind sand dunes a mile or so from the river, and standing out conspicuously against the desert (fig. 86) for, while much damaged by time and plundering, they are much larger than the tombs at Kurru. The first and largest structure at Nuri is the tomb of King Taharqa, the best known of the kings of the 25th Dynasty, who ruled over Egypt and has left many monuments there. It measures about 150 feet square and is the most prominent building on the site. Spreading from its base to north and south are the tombs of the queens of the Napatan royal family, and in a second group just

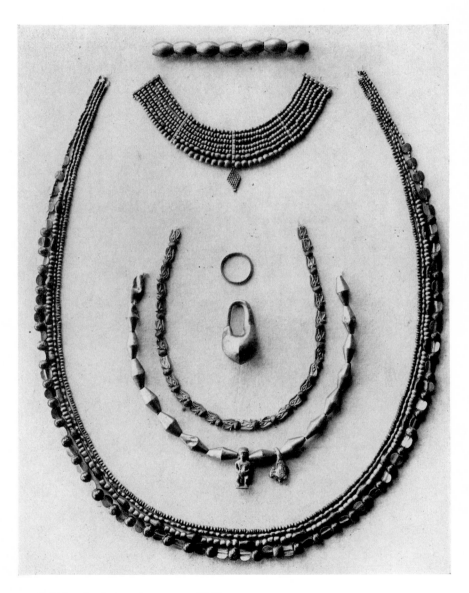

77. Gold jewelry from early graves at El Kurru.
ca. 800-700 B.C. *Expedition* (*some in Khartoum*).

78. The tomb of King Piankhy
at El Kurru, looking west.

79. The coffin-bench of a tomb
at El Kurru, with two bronze legs
for the funerary bed still
standing in their niches.

78

79

east of these are the pyramids of the other Napatan kings who ruled over the Land of Kush for some 350 years, from 690 to 337 B.C. The Harvard–Boston Expedition worked here during three winter seasons — 1916 to 1918, excavating the tombs of eighteen kings and fifty-four royal ladies, as well as several subsidiary buildings. This work has made possible the recovery of the names of many unknown kings and queens of Kush, their chronological order and relationship, and has clarified the history of the period, its cultural relationship to Egypt, and its gradual evolution away from the influence of its great northern neighbor.

At Kurru we saw how the ancient burial customs of Kush had been modified under the influence of Egyptian religion—how the tumulus form of structure had given way to the mastaba and pyramid, how human sacrifice had been given up and the use of shawabti figures had been taken over from Egypt, and how mummification, as proven by the presence of canopic jars, began to be practised. Only the use of a funerary bed instead of a coffin remained. In a few of the early tombs of women at Nuri the use of a funerary bed was evident. It seems as though the ladies living a sheltered life in the harem, were slower to change their habits than their men-folk, whose contacts with the world of ideas were more direct. But apart from this survival for the first generation or so, the burial customs at Nuri seem to have been completely Egyptian. From now on the dead were mummified and buried in stone sarcophagi or wooden coffins, accompanied by canopic jars and shawabti figures, and supplied with heart scarabs and the usual Egyptian amulets for protection against the perils of the next world. In some of the more important tombs we find also Egyptian inscriptions from the "Book of the Dead", stelae and offering-tables similar to those in use in Egypt at this time, in general a pretty complete adoption of Egyptian practices.

Of the many interesting objects which have come to us from Nuri, perhaps the series of shawabti figures are the most revealing. They were found in almost every tomb, were almost all inscribed, and it is from them primarily that we have learned the names of these people. In some tombs they were found in great profusion: those of King Taharqa alone numbered over a thousand, all of hard stone, and ranging in size from eight to thirty-two inches. When arranged in chronological order they show us two things of considerable significance. The earliest figures were beautifully made and are real works of art, but then we see a gradual change, a decline not so much in size, but rather in quality and in the

80. Gold collar of a queen of Shabako. D. 6¼ in. 25th Dynasty. From El Kurru. *Expedition.*

technical skill of their manufacture, and paralleling this change is a degradation in the inscriptions. The earliest of these are well written and grammatical-
ly correct, but in both respects the latest are quite pathetic in their apparent
ignorance of the Egyptian language.

Among the significant objects found at Nuri were a number of large stone
scarabs which we call heart-scarabs because they were placed in the mummy to
act as substitutes for the real heart. They were inscribed with one of the chapters from the Book of the Dead, including the name of the person for whom they
were made. I always think there is a rather pathetic human interest connected
with them. In the Egyptian conception of the hereafter, the dead, when he
came to judgment, had his heart weighed in the balance against a feather —
the symbol of truth. The text inscribed on these scarabs is a prayer that the

heart may be successful in this ordeal, and that no hostile testimony may be brought against it. One cannot help wondering too whether it was hoped that the heavy stone heart would tip the balance in favor of the dead against the feather of truth.

One of the most interesting of the major tombs of Nuri was the pyramid of King Aspelta who lived shortly after the 25th Dynasty while the Napatan Kingdom of Kush was still wealthy and near the high point of its artistic achievements. The pyramid still stands almost to its original height together with the remains of its chapel (fig. 87). The great stairway descending into the rock to the east led *via* a blocked doorway to three supulchral chambers cut out of the living rock under the pyramid. These were lined throughout with stone slabs inscribed with hieroglyphic funerary texts, and in the innermost room stood the great granite sarcophagus of the king which may now be seen in the crypt outside the Lecture Hall in the Museum. It weighs about fourteen tons, and had to be hauled up the stairway by our workmen and thence for a mile across sand dunes to the river, where a barge brought it to the railway on its long journey to Boston. The roofs of these subterranean chambers had collapsed anciently, apparently while the old plunderers were looting the tomb, and their hasty retreat may be the reason why a considerable number of fine objects were left behind by them. Outstanding among these, both to be seen in our Jewelry Room, were a graceful gold vessel with inscribed handle, and an alabaster vase with an ornamental gold rim and shoulder decorated in cloisonné enamel with a series of semi-precious stone pendants hung on little woven gold wire chains, a unique combination of the stone cutters' and goldsmiths' arts which though found badly damaged, has been successfully restored by our Research Laboratory (fig. 88). From the same tomb also came several pairs of gold tweezers which are still quite usable. From another rich burial at Nuri came a large silver disc mirror with four figures of gods forming its handle, and a golden figure of the winged goddess Isis which had formed part of the decoration of the king's mummy (fig. 89). Nuri yielded us many other interesting and beautiful objects which time will not allow me to describe here. The illustration which they furnish of the craftsmanship and artistic skill of the men who worked for these Napatan kings of Kush from the seventh to the fourth centuries B.C. can now be seen nowhere else in the world, for the share of our finds which went to the Sudan Government are not easily accessible pending the construction of an adequate museum in Khartoum.

82

81

81. Gold plated electrum handle of a mirror
of King Shabako. L. of handle 5⅜ in.
25th Dynasty. El Kurru. *Expedition.*

82. Blue-glazed faience amulets
from Queens' tombs at El Kurru.
25th Dynasty. *Expedition.*

83. Rock crystal and gold amulet:
head of the goddess Hathor. H. 2⅛ in.
25th Dynasty. El Kurru. *Expedition.*

83

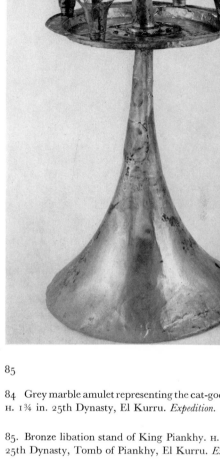

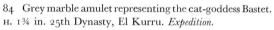

85

84   Grey marble amulet representing the cat-goddess Bastet. H. 1¾ in. 25th Dynasty, El Kurru. *Expedition.*

85. Bronze libation stand of King Piankhy. H. 2 ft. 8¼ in. 25th Dynasty, Tomb of Piankhy, El Kurru. *Expedition.*

84

86. View of the Pyramids of Nuri, looking west, before excavation.

87. The Pyramid of King Aspelta at Nuri, showing chapel
and cutting for entrance stairway. Looking southwest.

89

88

88. Alabaster vase with gold and enamel collar and mouth. H. 9¾ in. ca. 570 B.C. Tomb of Aspelta at Nuri. *Expedition.*

89. Sheet gold relief figure of winged Isis: from a mummy. L. 6½ in. ca. 520 B.C. From Pyramid 10 at Nuri. *Expedition.*

90. Silver mummy-trappings of a lady:
cleaned and restored.
ca. 600 B.C., from tomb S 85 at Meroë,
Expedition.

VIII Meroë and its Cemeteries

IN THE LAST CHAPTER we saw that the kings of Kush were buried in the great royal cemetery at Nuri up to shortly before 300 B.C. Now we journey on up the Nile to consider the last series of excavations of the Harvard–Boston Expedition in the royal cemeteries of Kush.

The city of Meroë lies on the east bank of the Nile between the Fifth and Sixth Cataracts, some 130 miles north of Khartoum. Since the Fourth Cataract above Napata has always been virtually impassable, the normal route from the latter place to Meroë lay south-east across the desert, a distance of about 150 miles. The earliest graves at Meroë go back to approximately 750 B.C., contemporary with Kurru, and the finds in its cemeteries show that the place was occupied continuously for about a thousand years. The city itself was investigated by the late Professor Garstang before our Expedition started work on its cemeteries, and his reports make it evident that it was a town of considerable importance in quite early Napatan times. Royal buildings were erected during the 25th Dynasty, and we believe that Meroë became an important administrative center and royal residence by 500 B.C. Certain it is that by about 300, if not sooner, it had become the capital of Kush, and from that time on the site of royal burial and focus of Kushite culture. Why this shift should have taken place must remain in part a matter of speculation, but I believe that there are a number of economic factors which had much to do with it.

From very early times Egypt was interested in the land of Kush and in the country further south in the Sudan because of the products to be obtained there. Kush was a primary source of gold — "The Gold Lands of Amon" — but the southland yielded many other things of value: cattle and hides, ebony, ivory, perfume oils, ostrich feathers, black slaves, to name only a few. In the Middle Kingdom Kerma above the Third Cataract was a major entrepôt for this traffic. During the New Kingdom, Napata became its center, lying as it does at the head of navigation just below the impassable Fourth Cataract. As long as Egypt remained a rich and powerful market—that is, throughout the New Kingdom— Kush derived profit and wealth from this traffic, which, coming down the Nile as far as Meroë, was brought by caravan across the desert, by-passing the Fourth Cataract, to Napata, whence it went down river again to Egypt. The two centers

91

92

91. View of Tomb S 85 as found
with burial in place.

92. Detail in S 85, showing silver
trappings of the Lady Mernua as found.

93. Alabaster ointment vase:
a bound antelope.
L. 7 in. Early Kushite, ca. 700 B.C.
Tomb W 609 at Meroë. *Expedition.*

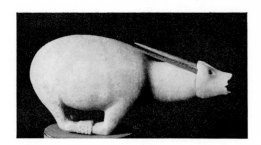

93

of Meroë and Napata had their economic raisons d'être, as transfer points on this trade route.

But beginning about 525 B.C. Egypt itself fell under the domination of the rising powers to the north, first Persia, then Greece and Rome; powers whose domination over Egypt never extended much beyond the First Cataract at Assuan. The new political orientation of Egypt brought with it a shift in the pattern of trade. Egypt, herself dominated, could no longer exert her influence in Kush. Trade with the south diminished and with it the sources of wealth for that land. Thus, there had inevitably to be a reorientation of the Kingdom of Kush. Napata lost importance as a trans-shipment point in the trade with Egypt, and Meroë gained in significance as the place to which the products of the south were brought by river. It should not be taken that the trade with Egypt ceased to exist; it undoubtedly did not. But I do believe that it diminished in importance as a major factor in the economy of Kush. Not only was Egypt now looking northward and enjoying a closer intimacy with the Mediterranean world and her neighbors to the north and east, but the political changes of this period meant that the security of transit between Egypt and Kush was no longer what it had been. And another factor must also be considered, and that is climate. The northern Sudan is virtually rainless and uninhabitable except where the Nile provided water for irrigation along its banks. But at approximately the level of the Fifth Cataract one comes into the country where there is an annual summer rainy season, where grass will grow after the rains, where cattle can be grazed and crops grown back from the river, and where above all thorn trees can grow. Since Meroë lies within this area it was a natural center for cattle raising as well as agriculture, but even more important was its proximity to

94

sources of wood. For in this region were extensive deposits of iron ore which could be rendered into the useful metal by heat, and here too was the source of charcoal for smelting. As in modern times the juxtaposition of iron ore and coal in the Ruhr in Europe and the Midlands in Britain have been the foundation of great industrial activity, so these factors made Meroë a center of iron working in ancient times, and still today the great slag heaps hard by the ruins of that city attest to the fact. Thus, the iron-working industry increased the importance of Meroë. Our knowledge is still too incomplete for us to know just how this product affected trade patterns. That there was considerable use of the metal locally is certain: its superiority over bronze for tools and weapons made this inevitable. We remain, however, in ignorance as to the extent to which it figured as an important item in trade with Egypt or with the primitive peoples further south, although it seems reasonable to assume both.

At Meroë we excavated three great cemeteries adjacent to the city, known as the South, North, and West Cemeteries. The earliest graves in the West Cemetery date back to the time of Kurru, and it was in continuous use for some thousand years until late Meroitic times. This was the burial place of the inhabitants of the city who were not kings and major queens, but it included tombs of secondary members of the royal family. The South Cemetery, started at the same time, remained in use until about 275 B.C. and contains the pyramids of two kings and six queens who lived just prior to that date. Then there was no more room in this necropolis and a new one was therefore established just north of it, known as the North Cemetery. Here are the tombs of the rulers of Meroë from this time until the final collapse of the Kingdom just before A.D. 340.

Before describing the work done in the cemeteries at Meroë and speaking of the finds, I think it will be interesting to revert for a moment to the matter of

94. View of the two royal cemeteries at Meroë: looking north to the North Cemetery with South Cemetery in foreground.

95. Detail in North Cemetery at Meroë, looking south.

95

the local burial practices which I have taken up in previous chapters. In the early tombs in the West and South Cemeteries we found many burials quite like those at Kurru, with the body resting on a bed and with no evidences of mummification. But side by side with them, and apparently of the same date, were many typical Egyptian graves containing mummified burials stretched out in coffins. I am convinced that here we had the tombs of Egyptians — scribes, minor officials of government, and skilled craftsmen brought up from Egypt to serve the Kushite nobility, who dying there were buried according to their own custom. And it is notable that these Egyptian graves were generally those of relatively poor people who took few possessions with them, whereas many of those buried according to Kushite practice were definitely rich and well supplied for their journey to the next world.

In discussing Nuri we saw that at the height of the Napatan Kingdom the burial customs of the royal family had become fully Egyptianized with hardly a trace of the earlier local practices, although at the end we found a great falling off in quality. In the royal tombs of Meroë, both in the South Cemetery and in the earlier burials of the North Cemetery, we find a continuation of these same practices. The custom of mummifying the dead continued and there were occasional examples of stone sarcophagi. But it is obvious that the use of Egyptian funerary texts had become an almost meaningless tradition and the language was no longer understood by the scribes who had become practically illiterate. As time went on the contents of the graves changed. The quality of workmanship deteriorated still further and things of Egyptian style were replaced by objects of local type, and also imports from Hellenized Alexandria such as bronzes of late Classical type, and glass beads and vessels of Greco-Roman wares. Then somewhere about the beginning of the first century A.D. we came upon a really startling development. We began to find occasional tombs with more than one burial. In these cases the owner had been placed in a wooden coffin, but near by were anywhere from one to four or five skeletons lying on the floor. In one tomb of a queen, among four subsidiary burials lay her maid clutching her mistress' jewelry in a little bag, and in one rather dreadful case it was obvious from the attitude of the skeleton that a servant had come to life after the tomb had been closed and had died of suffocation. This of course reminds us of the practice of human sacrifice which we had found at Kerma way back about 2000 B.C. and which had already been given up at Kurru. And we must conclude that, as the influence of civilized Egypt gradually faded from memory, the ancient barbaric

customs of Kush had begun to come back. That this appears actually to have
been the case is shown by a few very late tombs at Meroë, excavated near the
city by Professor Garstang and which are clearly to be dated to a time later
than the fall of Meroë. These burials were covered with circular mounds as at
Kerma, and in them too, the dead had been placed on beds and not in coffins.
And so we can feel quite sure that the immemorial customs of the inhabitants
of Kush eventually conquered the ideas and practices which came from contact with Egypt, and that that experience had no permanent effect as against
the all conquering conservatism of a primitive people.

Let me turn now to the things we found at Meroë and which enrich our collections here in Boston. As I have already said, the earlier tombs in the West
and South cemeteries were contemporary with those at Kurru and Nuri. One
of the richest of these which had not been plundered was a bed-burial which
contained a great quantity of bronze bowls, stone vases, and amulets. Among
these were some quite unique alabaster ointment jars representing a horned
antelope bound for sacrifice (fig. 93). The horns were made of slate and inserted
and the open mouth of the animal served as the mouth of the vase. By contrast
many conventional Egyptian-style burials had mummies equipped with bead
nets. In general, the beads and amulets were similar to those found at Kurru
(see figs. 77 and 82), and in one case at least we found an amulet at Meroë
which from the identical mold as a duplicate in one of the queen's tombs
at Kurru.

In the South Cemetery, and to be dated soon after the end of the 25th Dynasty, a very rich tomb was known as S 85, the burial chamber of which was
unplundered although nothing remained of the building above ground. It had
belonged to a lady of high rank by the name of Mernua. She lay encased in a
triple set of wooden anthropoid coffins upon a low bench in the center of the
room, and all about against the walls of the chamber stood the faience shawabti
figures from which her name was recovered (fig. 91). Within the coffins and
over the mummy itself had been placed a gilded silver mask, a broad collar,
winged scarab, and other figures (fig. 92), under which stretched a net of
faience and silver beads. These mummy trappings have been cleaned, repaired
and reconstructed in the Museum's Research Laboratory and are on view in
our Seventh Egyptian Gallery (fig. 90), where the really beautifully modelling
of the mask may be appreciated.

The view (fig. 94) of the great royal pyramids of the Meroitic Kingdom of

Kush in the South and North Cemeteries is an impressive one for, unlike the earlier tombs, they are relatively well-preserved and have in many cases retained much of their original appearance (fig. 95). They yielded many small things of fine quality which are to be seen in our galleries, objects which are of peculiar interest to the art historian for they reflect the varied influences which affected Meroitic culture. Foremost among these was that of Egypt itself, albeit modified and distorted during generations of relative isolation which produced a fusing of native African with classic Egyptian which we call Meroitic art. But along with that we see the clear effect of Hellenistic Greek and later Roman art, coming to Meroë via Alexandria, partly by means of actual imports, perhaps partly by local imitation. A few examples will illustrate what I mean. The earliest case of import we found was from a relatively small tomb in the South Cemetery of about 400 B.C. This was a plastic rhyton representing an Amazon on horseback, signed by the Athenian potter Sotades, and hence attributable to Athens about 450 B.C. (fig. 96). It is a magnificent example of Greek Attic work and one of our great treasures. How it found its way to Meroë we can only guess — perhaps bought by a princely art lover, or possibly a royal gift from a foreign envoy to the Meroitic court. A number of other objects found at Meroë and dated to the end of the first century B.C. or early in the succeeding century, are clearly Alexandrian or Roman in style and very probably also imported, though they may possibly have been made by Hellenistic craftsmen working at Meroë. Such is the fine bronze head of Dionysos (fig. 97), a bronze lamp embellished with the fore-part of a horse, (fig. 98), a silver strainer with handles representing the heads and necks of geese, (fig. 99), and a silver goblet with handles, (fig. 100). But perhaps the most remarkable find of this class which came from the North Cemetery was the beautiful and delicate silver footed cup shown in fig. 101. We shall never know from which tomb this came for it was found miraculously intact wedged in between heavy stone blocks tumbled from the pyramids. It had doubtless fallen from the bag in which some ancient thief was making off with his loot. While on this subject of foreign influence we should not forget the many evidences of the popularity of Roman glass at Meroë. We found many examples of fine imperial Roman glass vessels which are unfortunately too fragmentary for exhibition but nevertheless of no little importance for the study of wares and techniques. In addition, the tombs yielded Roman glass beads in great variety, including many in millefiori glass of which fig. 102 shows examples.

96. Attic Plastic Rhyton found at Meroë,
H. 13⅜ in. Greek ca. 450 B.C., from Tomb S 24 at Meroë.
Expedition.

97. Bronze head of Dionysos.
H. 5⅛ in. First Century A.D.,
from Pyramid N 5 at Meroë. *Expedition.*

98. Bronze lamp. H. 8¼ in. Late 1st Century A.D.
From Pyramid N 18 at Meroë. *Expedition.*

99. Silver strainer. L. 8⅜ in. ca. 290 B.C.
From Pyramid S 3 at Meroë. *Expedition.*

100. Silver cup with handles. H. 6⅝ in.
1st Century A.D., from Meroë. *Expedition.*

97

98

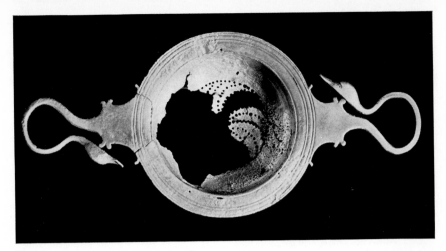

99

100

One of the most interesting objects from Meroë is a large bronze lamp which was found lying at the base of the stair leading to the burial chambers of an important tomb in the North Cemetery, (fig. 103). As far as research can tell us this object is of a hitherto unknown type. The body of the lamp stands on a foot and has a rather long projecting spout opposite which rises a large flame-guard in the form of an acanthus leaf. Although it has a loop handle behind the flame-guard it is also provided with a stem terminating in a hook in the form of a griffon's head, by which it could be hung. The stem, which is of iron, and the hook are not vertical, but inclined at such an angle that the lamp would hang from it in a horizontal position. Now this form of lamp is unique, but it also has other points of interest. Although the body of the lamp itself is of Classical form, as are also the acanthus flame-guard and the griffon's head hook, it was certainly of local manufacture. The back of the flame-guard bears an incised inscription in the Meroitic cursive script, probably the name of the maker or owner, and cast in relief on the lamp proper is a Meroitic heraldic device which we have found on objects of various kinds in the royal tombs and which I believe to be the special mark placed on objects intended for the Meroitic royal tomb equipment. Thus this lamp, clearly of Classical inspiration, was quite certainly made right here at Meroë.

In our Jewelry Room is a collection of gold and silver signet rings which came out of Meroitic tombs, one of the largest groups of the kind in the world. Others from the same source are in Khartoum. They bear designs in intaglio which are worthy of notice. Some are clearly of Egyptian inspiration, carved with various representations of Egyptian gods and goddesses or of emblems associated with them. Others are strictly Meroitic — the ruler seated on a throne, or the Meroitic lionheaded god of war. But a few are of Greek design, notably one with a Greek inscription and a particularly attractive ring bearing a figure of Athena armed with helmet, spear, and shield, and holding a little figure of the Winged Victory in her outstretched hand (fig. 104).

I have already said that Meroë lay within the rain belt and that the country furnished grazing for cattle. There is considerable evidence that cattle raising was an important occupation there, as indeed it is today. We have found the skeletons of cows sacrificed in the tombs and associated with them quite frequently were bronze bells, of which we have a number in the Museum. One in particular tells us how these bells were used, for it bears on its sides the representation of a cow wearing just such a bell around her neck (fig. 105). These

101. Silver goblet with relief scene.
H. 4⅛ in. ca. 50 B.C.
From North Cemetery at Meroë.
Expedition.

102. Millefiori glass beads.
ca. ⅜ in. square. 1st Century A.D.
From Tomb W 308 at Meroë.
Expedition.

101

102

104

105 a

103. Bronze hanging lamp. H. overall 22¾ in. 2nd Century A.D. From Pyramid N 29 at Meroë. *Expedition.*

104. Group of gold signet rings from Meroë. Meroitic Period. *Expedition (some in Khartoum).*

105 a & b. Bronze bell with incised figure of a cow (105b). H. 2½ in. Middle First Century A.D. From Pyramid N 15 at Meroë. *Khartoum.*

b

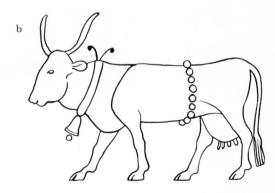

106. Silver ornamental plaques from leather trappings (harness?).
Late 1st Century A.D. From Tombs N 16 and N 18 at Meroë. *Expedition*.

107. Bronze quiver for poisoned arrows. L. 16⅝ in. 2nd Century A.D.
From Tomb W 122 at Meroë. *Expedition*.

bells were, of course, of local manufacture. Also clearly the work of Meroitic craftsmen were a number of silver plaques made as ornaments to be attached, possibly, to leather trappings now lost. A number of these are in the Museum: medallions with finely modelled lion heads, and rectangular plaques showing bounding lions or deities of several sorts (fig. 106). One product of the Meroitic metal worker which we found is very interesting and is illustrated in fig. 107. It is a bronze cylinder closed at one end and with a tightly fitting hinged cover at the other. It is provided with a chain for carrying over the shoulder, and at one end has several little bells suspended from chains so that they would ring whenever the cylinder was moved. When the lid was opened the cylinder was found to contain a bundle of very small light arrows, their tips showing marked discoloration. This was a quiver for hunting with poisoned arrows, and the tightly fitting lid and the warning bells were intended to protect the user from careless handling of these dangerous weapons.

Perhaps the most characteristic class of object found at Meroë was the jewelry. Many examples are shown in one of our galleries, among them an interesting group from the tomb of a queen which had been buried in the keeping of her sacrificed maid who had them in a little bag clutched to her breast. Here we found six pairs of ear-rings, two pairs of gold and carnelian bracelets, one necklace made of multiple strands of gold, carnelian, and blue glass beads, two necklaces of gold ball beads, a fourth necklace of rather coarse gold and glass beads, three finger-rings and a bronze mirror. The bracelets were especially fine for they had been strung on gold wire and were entirely intact, it being only necessary to wash the dirt from them to restore their original appearance (fig. 108). In addition to the ear-rings already mentioned there were several other types, including large disc-shaped ones, some of which showed quite elaborate designs worked out in cloisonné enamel. Necklaces and bracelets also occurred in great variety, some of them made up of multiple gold elements representing uraeus serpents, rams' heads and other amuletic motifs (fig. 109).

The profusion and variety of Meroitic jewelry is well illustrated by the costuming of a queen depicted on the wall of her chapel in the North Cemetery, a relief which dates to the last quarter of the first century b.c. (fig. 110). This truly mountainous royal lady is shown positively weighed down by her ornaments as she sits in state on her lion throne. The many reliefs from the pyramid chapels at Meroë are of great interest, but they remain on the site and are difficult to illustrate by photography because they have been very badly weathered

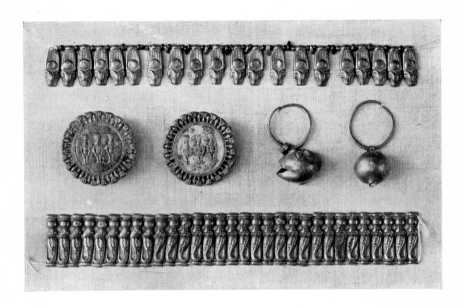

108. Meroitic gold jewelry, including ear-studs. D. of largest 1½ in. 1st Century A.D.
From graves in the West Cemetery at Meroë. *Expedition.*

by time and can only be adequately seen in drawings. The best of them are well
executed in a style which owes much to Egyptian tradition, but yet is distinctively Meroitic. Like everything else at Meroë the later examples show marked
degeneration both in style and workmanship, reflecting the loss of vigor which
marked the later phases of a dying culture. Two examples must suffice to illustrate the point. The first comes from the scenes at the top of a great stone stela
found at Barkal and now in the Museum (fig. 111). Here in a crudely incised
scene the king drags a captive before Amon and makes an offering to two other
gods, while above his name is written in a curious travesty of ancient Egyptian
known as Meroitic hieroglyphs. Below is a band of bound captives, and the
lower part of the stone is taken up with a long inscription in the cursive script
of the Meroitic language which as yet cannot be fully understood by scholars.
Finally, we have an offering stone of a late type depicting in crude relief the
deities, Anubis and Nephthys, pouring a libation for the deceased, whose name
and a funerary formula are inscribed around the border in the Meroitic language (fig. 112).

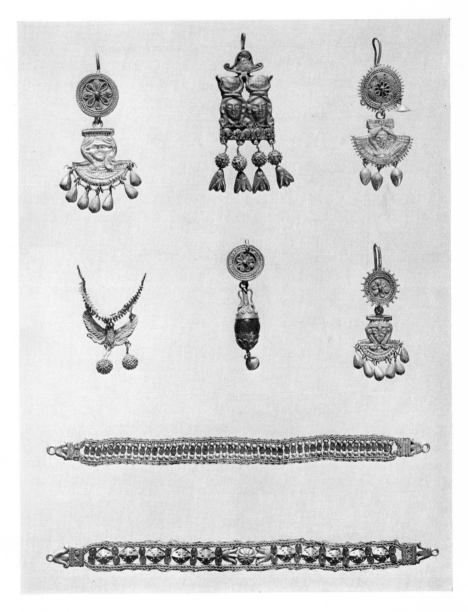

109. Group of gold and carnelian bracelets and ear-rings. L. of bracelets 5⅝ in. Mid 1st Century B.C. From Pyramid W 5 at Meroë. Partly in Boston and Khartoum.

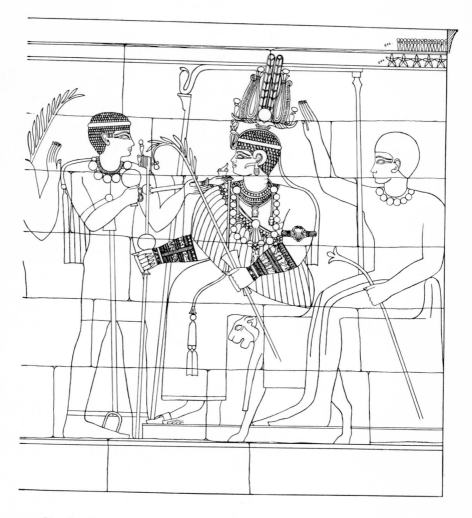

110. Line drawing: a queen of Meroë enthroned. ca. 20 B.C.
From a wall relief in Pyramid N 6 at Meroë.

111. Grey granite stela of King Tanyidamani. H. 5 ft. 3 in. ca. 120 B.C.
From Temple of Amon at Barkal. *Expedition.*

112. Granite offering-stone with cursive Meroitic inscription.
L. 14½ in. 1st to 2nd Century B.C.
From Tomb W 19 at Meroë. *Expedition.*

III

112

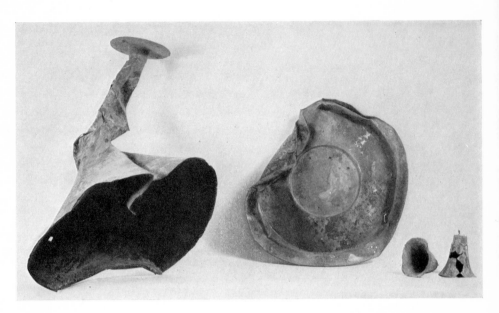

113 a

113 b

113 a & b. Parts of the Libation Stand
of Piankhy as found
(See fig. 85).

IX Observations on Egyptian Art

WE HAVE in the foregoing eight chapters discussed the Egyptian collection in Boston, its beginnings and early growth; and then the work of the Egyptian Expedition with the resulting increase both in size and distinction of the collection, not to mention the great contributions to our knowledge of ancient Egypt and the Sudan resulting from excavations.

In this final chapter I must touch briefly on another aspect of our work. In the course of excavation we find not only beautiful objects sufficiently intact to be exhibited in the Museum, but also many broken and incomplete things, or pieces so adversely affected by the passage of time that they would have little meaning if shown in the condition in which they were found. We are fortunate here in Boston in having one of the finest and most complete departments of restoration and research in the country, under the able direction of William J. Young, and the Department has made frequent use of his talents and skills, not only in bringing ancient objects back to usefulness but also in studying other problems, and especially in deciding whether objects offered to us are genuine antiquities or clever modern forgeries.

I have spoken in an earlier chapter of the painstaking work done in the restoration of the silver mummy-trappings of the Princess Mernua from Meroë, a lengthy process requiring prolonged electrolytic consolidation of the corroded metal and very skillful and delicate brazing together of fragments (see figs. 92 and 93). Similar skill by Mr. Young and his staff made possible the restoration (see fig. 84) of the twisted and broken fragments (fig. 113) of the bronze libation stand found crushed by rock falls in the tomb of Piankhy at Kurru. An example of what may be done by electrolysis is furnished by the bronze aegis acquired by the Museum in 1931 in a shockingly corroded condition. After many months of treatment it emerged with its elaborate inlaid decoration once more clearly visible (fig. 114). Another task frequently undertaken by the Research Laboratory has several times resulted in making fragmentary and incomplete stone statues suitable for exhibition in the galleries. Such a case was presented by a group of alabaster fragments from Giza which, by skillful fitting together and restoration of the missing parts, became a very distinguished member of the company of Old Kingdom figures shown in our great First Egyptian Gallery (fig. 115).

114 a & b. Bronze Aegis of Isis. H. 10⅞ in. 22nd Dynasty? *Adelia Cotton Williams Fund.*
a. before treatment; b. after treatment.

115 a. Fragments of an alabaster statuette of Khnum-Baf.
5th Dynasty from Giza. *Expedition.*

115 b. The statuette of Khnum-Baf restored. H. 2 ft. 2½ in.

114 a   b

115 a   b

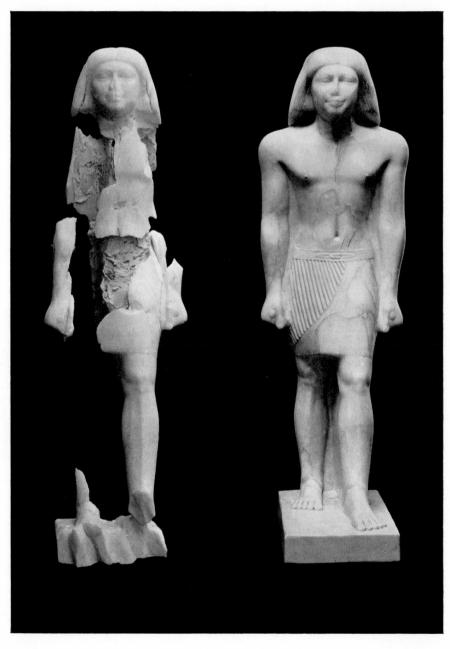

116. Painted limestone stela (fig. 41): Detail in ultra-violet light.

117. Modern Sudanese girl grinding corn.

118. Limestone figure of a servant grinding corn. L. 12¼ in. 6th Dynasty. From Giza. *Expedition.*

Many other techniques are employed in the laboratory, especially in aiding the Department in determining the authenticity of objects which it may have under consideration. These procedures range all the way from microscopic examination through X-ray and ultra-violet inspection, to chemical analysis and spectrography. These tests are helpful in re-enforcing the judgment of the Department based on the knowledge and experience of the trained archaeologist. Seldom in my experience have these technical examinations gone contrary to that judgment. In fact, in a number of instances the doubts of the Curator, based on stylistic evaluations, have been shown to be justified by them. Finally, the work in the laboratory may be very helpful in other ways. One striking example shows how ultra-violet light may sometimes make legible painted inscriptions which are quite invisible in normal illumination. Fig. 41 is a normal photograph of a stela of the First Intermediate Period, which shows two children at the feet of the principal figures. Fig. 116 is a photograph in ultra-violet light of this detail, in which the names of the two children, originally painted in green color on the stone and now quite invisible to the eye, are once more made legible.

With all its conventions, Egyptian art is realistic in the sense that it portrays

117

118

119. Copy of a relief scene in the Tomb of Ptah-hotep at Sakkara
(from a squeeze in the Museum of Fine Arts). 5th Dynasty.

concrete facts in a matter of fact way. We cannot always realize this, largely because we are seldom able to visualize the facts which were so familiar to the
Egyptian artist. Occasionally, however, we can do this because so many of the
practices of ancient Egypt still survive today. I have found two examples from
the present day which serve to illustrate my point. The first is a photograph of
a modern Sudanese girl grinding grain in a stone mortar (fig. 117), which is
exactly what is represented on a limestone figure of the Old Kingdom in the
Museum (fig. 118). The second and more striking example is illustrated in figs.
119 and 120, the first of which, from a relief in a 5th Dynasty tomb at Sakkara,
shows boys playing a game which would be difficult to interpret without the
photograph of Arab boys in Jordan doing exactly the same thing.

Finally, I want briefly to try and express a few ideas of mine on Egyptian art
and culture as inspired by this great collection. I suppose no other civilization
that we know of has shown so little change in the idiom of the artist over so long
a period. Take Europe for example: the stylized paintings of the Byzantine period
with their stiff forms and rudimentary modelling gave place to Giotto, then to
the forerunners of Raphael. By the High Renaissance, the representation of a

120. Photograph of Arab boys high-jumping. (after photograph published in MFA Bulletin XXV (1937) p. 54 by permission of the American Colony, Jerusalem).

three-dimensional world in full light and shade and in realistic perspective had replaced earlier idioms. Later still, we have seen first the development of complete realism and then the revolt against such painting in impressionism, post-impressionism, and today in surrealism. All this has taken place in less than a thousand years. The whole history of Egyptian Art covers approximately three times as long a period, yet the changes in its methods of representation — in the idiom employed by the artist and understood by his patrons — are hardly perceptible to most of us.

There are many reasons for this. First, the essential isolation of Egyptian civilization, protected throughout its formative stages from contact with the outside world. With deserts to east and west, with the barrier of the Nile cataracts to the south and the sea to the north, the narrow fertile valley of Egypt was to its early inhabitants a world unchanging and undisturbed. The idiom — the style of Egyptian art — seems to have been evolved at an early period of simplicity, by a people with a very practical and direct outlook on life. They learned to represent the facts of nature as they saw them, or rather as they knew them to be, in what seems to us an almost childlike directness. Take for example, the

121. Relief Figure of the Treasury Official Nofer. H. of figure 2 ft. 9 in. 4th Dynasty. From Giza. *Expedition.*

human figure as represented in relief and painting (fig. 121). It did not look as it would appear to the eye from any particular point of view. Rather it took each element in the figure in what seemed to the artist its most characteristic aspect — the face in profile so as to show the shape of the nose, mouth and chin; the eye as seen from in front in order to show its characteristic shape; the shoulders also from front view so as to indicate their projection on either side. The combination of these different points of view in a single figure gave a distorted visual impression, but nevertheless did represent the facts of what the figure is like. These representations are more like explanatory diagrams than representations in our sense but, to my mind, they are not disturbing, partly because I am used to them, and perhaps also because the Egyptians had an innate gift for moderation and for design. By the time we find preserved works of art, soon after 3000 B.C., they were no longer experimenting with new conceptions; they had established their idiom and it had proved itself satisfactory and was retained with but little change for 3000 years.

Then, too, we should always remember that the Egyptian artist was a crafts-man working not to express himself, but to meet a very practical and utilitarian demand. At the outset certainly, and for the most part throughout Egyptian his-tory, works of art were produced in the service of religion or of funerary beliefs. The figure of the god — or of the king who was a living god — was a necessary cult image or object of worship. The funerary statue was a habitation for the spirit in the afterlife, and the relief scenes of activities of daily life were not so much pictures in our sense as magic reproductions of fact and action which would be imbued with life in the hereafter to be of use to the deceased. When we see a picture of a man playing draughts with his wife, or sitting before a pile of good things to eat, the picture was thought of as ensuring him those pleasures in the next world. It may also be pointed out that it is almost an axiom to the stu-dent of manners and customs of the past, that man is extremely conservative in matters of religion and funerary practice. We still use archaic English, or the dead language, Latin, in the ritual of our churches, although both have been discarded in our daily lives. When art is employed in the service of religion, the tendency to conservatism is a powerful factor. As far as we can tell art was anony-mous; we know the names of hardly any artists and can rarely recognize the work of any individual. All we can do is to recognize the style of a period, and sometimes of a locality in that period; for to the trained eye there are slight but perceptible differences between the work of the Old Kingdom and the later phases of Egyptian culture, though often they are not easy to detect. These differences lie sometimes in changes in costume as styles changed, however slowly, sometimes only in the spirit of treatment. These subtle variations have a definite relation to the changes in the history of the country.

The Old Kingdom may be characterized as a time of complete concentration of power and wealth at court and with it a focusing of talent of every kind in the service of the king and government. Only at Giza and Sakkara, which were the cemeteries of the capital, Memphis, is work of high quality found. But this concentration of power in the royal family led to the dissipation of Egypt's wealth on the production of such economically useless things as pyramids, tombs, and temples to the gods, on an utterly fantastic scale; not on public works which would increase the productive capacity of the country. By the end of the 6th Dynasty this led to a collapse of ordered government and to a period of anarchy and poverty which we call the First Intermediate Period. During that time the production of works of art seems to have ceased, and we find only such travesties of erstwhile skill as the stelae from tombs in Middle Egypt, such as I referred to in Chapter V (see fig. 41). And yet the technical skills of the great schools of sculpture of the Old Kingdom do not seem to have been entirely forgotten, for with the return of law and order in the Middle Kingdom, the Egyptians again produced great works of art. A few important architectural works remain from this period: the brick pyramids (no longer stone) of the 12th Dynasty kings near Memphis, the 11th Dynasty tomb-temple of Deir el Bahari at Thebes, now for the first time the capital city, and a beautiful little shrine at Karnak recently rebuilt from the original blocks which had been re-used in one of the later pylons at Karnak — these are among the few monuments we have left. The political anarchy of the First Intermediate Period was replaced by government under locally powerful barons in various parts of the country, and by the beginning of the Middle Kingdom these nobles were acknowledging the superiority of the most powerful of their number, the princes of Thebes, who became the kings of the 11th and 12th Dynasties. This was a feudal age with centers of power and culture up and down the country, acknowledging the over-lordship of the crown at Thebes, and, therefore, art was no longer confined exclusively to the capital and court, and we find in the provinces such magnificent examples as our painted coffin from Bersheh, and the statue of the Lady Sennuwy at Kerma in an outpost far off in the Sudan (see fig. 64).

The Middle Kingdom gave way to the Second Intermediate Period which has left us no major works of art. It was a period of internal anarchy and, for the first time in Egyptian experience, major foreign invasion and occupation. An Asiatic people, known to us as the Hyksos, ruled in Lower Egypt and there was war between them and the princes of Thebes.

At length the Thebans of the 17th Dynasty drove them out and pursued them into Palestine, and thus founded the New Kingdom. The 18th and 19th Dynasties lasted for more than 350 years. Ushered in by successful military action against foreigners, the New Kingdom rulers turned isolated Egypt into a world empire. Her borders were expanded as far as Asia Minor and the Euphrates, and to the south far into the Sudan. Tribute from the conquered peoples poured into Egypt and produced opulence and luxury never before known, and intimate contact with the outside world could not fail to have its effect on Egyptian thought, culture, and art. The products of New Kingdom art reflect these influences. Albeit the forms and subject matter remain essentially the same, there is a new spirit; luxury, sophistication, and ostentation mark much of New King-

dom work, and perhaps a certain vulgarity may be detected from time to time. A degree of naive directness has given way to a self-conscious striving for effect. There is a change of spirit which one might perhaps compare to the difference between the Italian painting of Giotto and his followers and that of the High Renaissance, and yet there is little change in subject matter and idiom.

With the end of the New Kingdom we enter on a long period of decline in power. Egypt's old energy seems to have worn itself out. The empire fell apart and foreign tribute ceased. Egypt was living on her great past. The power of Pharaoh, which formerly had been supreme, became now secondary to that of the High Priest of Amon, the great national god. A conservative, power-loving priesthood, self-seeking and trading on the superstitions of the people, was a deadening influence. Art tended to become stereotyped and wooden, though retaining a high degree of technical skill, and the works of the late period are with few exceptions uninspired. When the country was so weakened that the virile Sudanese kings of the 25th Dynasty were able to impose their rule upon it, they seem to have brought with them a renewal of vitality and, for a time during the 25th and 26th Dynasties, there was a period of revival when a certain amount of life returned to Egyptian art, especially in portrait sculpture. But this was the dying flicker of the flame; thereafter domination by Persia, then by Greece under the Ptolemies, and finally by Rome, brought the end of ancient Egyptian civilization as we know it. Hellenistic Greek interest in detailed modelling of the human figure is reflected in the sculpture of Ptolemaic Egypt, and Roman interest in realistic portraiture played its part in the final phase. Only in Kush, far removed and isolated from the main stream of the interplay of competing cultures, did the old traditional style continue with ever decreasing skill and increasing barbarism long after traditional art had disappeared from its native land.